CONTENTS

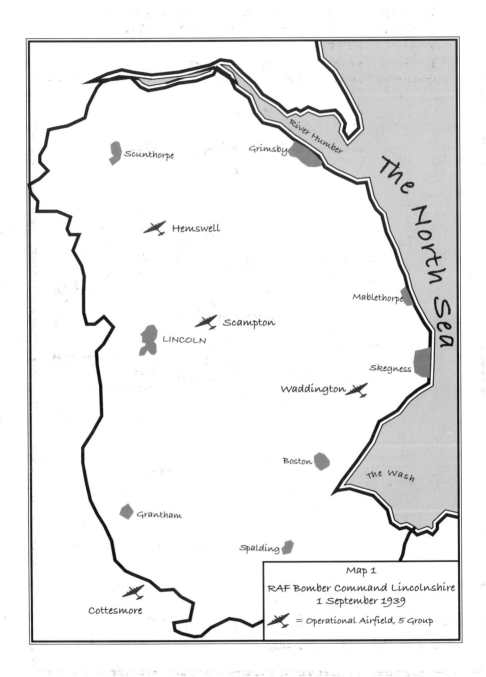

Map 1

RAF Bomber Command Lincolnshire
1 September 1939

 = Operational Airfield, 5 Group

The publishers apologise for the fact that several Bomber Command airfields, shown in the maps on pages 4 and 5, are incorrectly positioned.

The map below reflects their proper location.

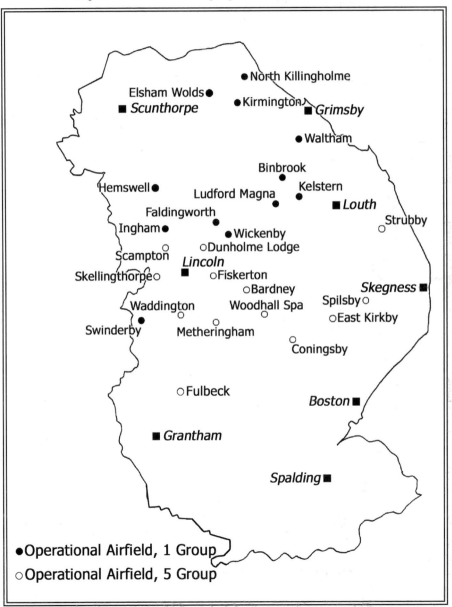

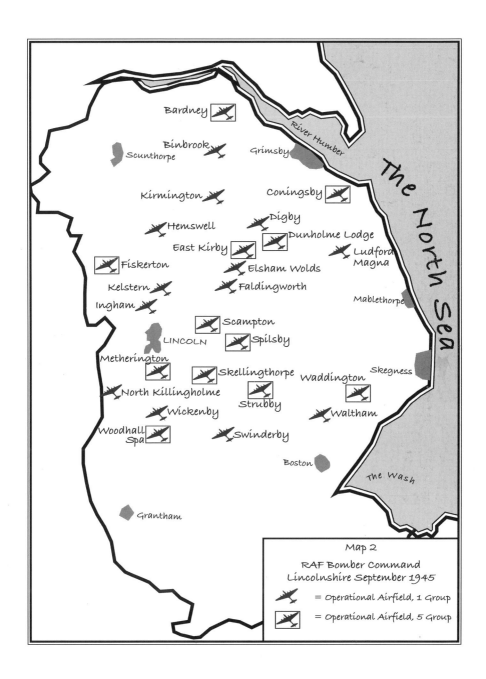

Map 2

RAF Bomber Command
Lincolnshire September 1945

= Operational Airfield, 1 Group

= Operational Airfield, 5 Group

Preface

My father never really spoke very much about his time in Bomber Command. He volunteered on 4 September 1939, though he was not actually called up until a few weeks later. He served through most of 1940 in Bomber Command before transferring to the Air Ministry in London where he spent the rest of the war.

I gathered a few anecdotes over the years – such as the time his airfield was strafed by a Junkers 88 and he was very slightly injured, and the many times he had stood outside the control tower waiting for an aircraft that would never return. I know that he thought this the worst part. Men that he knew and counted as friends climbed into aircraft, flew off, and did not come back. And often those left behind never found out what had happened to their comrades.

Only once do I recall my father getting worked up about his time with the RAF. It must have been in the 1970s sometime, and we were watching a television programme about valuing antiques and collectors' items or some such. One member of the public had brought in letters relating to the wartime RAF.

The expert, who was quite young, picked out a few with famous names – they had a letter from Guy Gibson of Dambusters fame, I recall – and valued them, then airily waved the rest aside. He said, quite confidently, that many of the letters were not really written by the men whose signatures they carried. He picked one up. 'These letters to next of kin about men who were killed or missing,' he said, 'they are just standard form letters run up by a secretary or clerk. The squadron leaders never wrote these themselves.'

My father was furious. I don't think I ever saw him so angry. After ranting at the screen for a few moments, he turned to me.

'Now listen,' he said. 'That man is talking rubbish. He thinks he is being clever, but he is insulting the memory of my friends who died for this country. I'm going to tell you what really happened because I was there and I saw it. My squadron leaders [I think father served under two, the first being shot down] always wrote these letters themselves. They wouldn't let anyone else near them. They said that it was the very least that they could do for the poor men who had been killed or were missing – write a personal letter to the relatives telling them what had happened and saying something

A cartoon drawn by the author's father showing the officers of his Bomber Squadron in July 1940. Most of the men shown here were killed during the war.

about how their boy had behaved at the squadron.'

My father lent forward in his chair.

'I recall one raid that went very badly wrong in 1940 when our squadron was out bombing the invasion barges. We lost a lot of aircraft and a lot of men. An hour or two after the survivors got back, I had to take a note about something to the CO. I knocked on the door, but there was no reply. I thought he must be out of his office, so I went in to leave the note on his desk. But he was not out. He was there all right – slumped over the desk in tears writing those letters to next of kin.'

He flicked an angry glance at the television. 'And that young fool says they were form letters.' My father glared at the screen for a second or two, then said, 'All those young men. Those poor young men.' Abruptly he got up and left the room. I think he did not want me to see him cry.

So for my father, and for all his comrades whether they returned or not, I am proud to write this book about the Heroes of Bomber Command.

Finally, a book such as this cannot possibly be the work of just one person.

There are many people I would like to thank, but special mention must be made of: Squadron Leader George Hatton for loaning me his invaluable *History of 153 Squadron*; Mr Peter Scawly for allowing me access to the wonderful RAF Metherington Museum; Mr Bob Baxter for his invaluable advice and for access to his photo library, and for his highly informative website: http://www.bomber-command.info/; Mr David Fell and the RAF Elsham Wolds Association for access to their collection of files, information and photos – and for their absorbing website: http://elshamwolds.50g.com/home.html; Noel Ryan for his expertise on the current state of the old RAF airfields in Lincolnshire and his great website: www.oldairfields.fotopic. net; Cobey Lilley for the map reading; my father for his inspiration; and my wife for her patience.

Rupert Matthews

A group of officers awaiting the return of a squadron from a night raid during the autumn of 1940. All too often the aircraft failed to return.

Introduction

When war came to Lincolnshire in September 1939, it was already a bomber county so far as the RAF was concerned. And a bomber county it was to remain throughout the six long years of conflict. But it was never intended that the county would serve as the base for a massive bombing campaign, as in fact happened. The RAF initially had very different ideas. To understand events in Lincolnshire, it is necessary to understand what was expected of the men who would fly from the county.

The crews of two Hampdens pose for an Air Ministry publicity photo beside their aircraft at an unidentified 5 Group airfield.

In 1934 the British government had decided to end its policy of defence cut backs that had seen the RAF shrink from 188 operational and 194 training squadrons in 1919 to just 16 front line squadrons. Prompted by the rapid growth of the German Luftwaffe, and the equally impressive Japanese and Italian air forces, the government began to build up the air force, with the aim of reaching 75 squadrons by March 1939, a target later uprated to 112 squadrons, of which 53 were to be bomber squadrons.

It was unfortunate for the crews of Bomber Command based in Lincolnshire, and elsewhere, that the rapid expansion of the force was based on a number of assumptions that turned out to be completely mistaken.

The first was that Britain would have France as an ally in any war against Germany. When the 'Phoney War' ended in May 1940 France collapsed so suddenly and completely that her air force was of no practical use to anybody except the Germans, who appropriated French aircraft for themselves. Unexpectedly the RAF had to face the Luftwaffe alone and unaided. The numbers of operational bomber squadrons were quite inadequate for the task they were abruptly handed.

A second assumption wiped out just as effectively by the French surrender concerned the performance of the aircraft. Strategists of the

1930s envisaged a repeat performance of the Great War. It was assumed that most of Bomber Command would be based at airfields in France and would be used to attack targets only a short distance beyond the front line. Even those aircraft designed to penetrate deep into Germany had a limited range. When France fell, the bomber crews found themselves faced with flying the long haul from Lincolnshire to Germany. Most aircraft simply did not have the range.

Finally, there was the fatal assumption that 'the bomber will always get through'. It was thought that the modern bombers of the later 1930s could fly fast enough to evade most enemy fighters, and had enough defensive armament to beat off attacks by those that did manage to intercept the raids. This fallacy would be cruelly dispelled by the early combats with the superb German fighters.

And because it was thought the bomber could 'get through', all the navigation and bomb-aiming equipment was designed for use in daylight. When the men flying from Lincolnshire switched to night raids for their own protection, they found themselves devoid of reliable navigation equipment and bombing almost blind.

Thus the basic purpose of Bomber Command was effectively impossible to achieve when war actually came. The RAF had designed its bomber force to hit an enemy hard and fast. It was to dominate the skies over enemy territory, raining death and destruction onto enemy troops and war industry alike. The men who had built up Bomber Command in the 1930s honestly believed that the bomber force alone could win a war. They thought that by pounding the enemy's armed forces and war factories, it could cripple any country's ability to wage war.

It was with these handicaps both in equipment and strategic thinking that the men of Bomber Command, Lincolnshire, went to war in 1939. With hindsight it is almost unbelievable that Lincolnshire's squadrons managed to achieve anything. But achieve things they did. The men struggled to take the war to the enemy as best they could. And as the months and years passed, lessons were learned. The crews were trained to fight a new style of air war, and the aircraft were built to match their needs.

By the end of the war, Bomber Command in Lincolnshire was one of the most modern, effective and tightly knit fighting forces anywhere in the world. Again and again the men serving in this command had shown themselves to be capable of astonishing feats of arms. They were, without any doubt, heroes.

Chapter 1

Lincolnshire Goes to War

Bomber Command's 5 Group, based in Lincolnshire, was lucky in 1939 that it had two of the finest airmen of the war on its strength. Throughout the conflict, the thinking of these two men would have a profound impact on the bomber force in the county, and on how it was to perform.

The first was Arthur Travers Harris who, when war broke out, was the commanding officer of 5 Group. Although he was later to be widely known as 'Bomber' Harris, the tough, taciturn officer was at this point rather better known for his enthusiasm for mine-laying.

Born in 1892, Harris had moved to Rhodesia (now Zimbabwe) in 1910 in search of adventure and a fortune. He tried his hand at gold mining, wagon driving and cattle driving before getting a job on a remote tobacco farm. When news arrived at his settlement in 1914 that war had broken out, Harris at once volunteered to serve in the 1st Rhodesian Regiment as a bugler. He spent the following months footslogging through the African bush as the British colonies went to war against the German colonies.

When the colonial campaigns were over, Harris volunteered for service outside Africa. Determined never again to march to war, he transferred to the fledgling Royal Flying Corps. He proved to be a natural pilot, his instructor passing him fit for a solo flight after just 30 minutes in the air. Harris spent the remainder of the war as a fighter pilot guarding London from Zeppelin raids, interspersed with spells on the Western Front. After the war, Harris gained a promotion to Squadron Leader, which involved changing to flying bombers and to being stationed in India. After some years there, Harris returned to Britain to take command of 58 Squadron, which he trained so well that they won the RAF bombing championship and logged more night-flying hours than the rest of the RAF put together.

Harris then moved to the Air Ministry where he was put in charge of Operations and developing new weapons. It was here that Harris began the research programme that would eventually lead to the production of the mighty four-engined bombers of the later war years. Of more immediate use, he sponsored the development of a marine mine that could be dropped from an aircraft in enemy waters. In 1938 Harris was promoted to the rank of Air Vice Marshal and sent to command the RAF in Palestine and Transjordan. The dry heat had a terrible effect on Harris's health, so he was brought back to Britain to take command of 5 Group.

Harris was a supremely capable airman who had a sound and instinctive grasp of air combat. Throughout his career he was determined that his men would have the best equipment and training that was possible, and he was dismissive of new fangled ideas until they proved their worth. In part, this gave Harris a reputation for being rather old-fashioned and doctrinaire. This was far from the truth. It was simply that he knew the dangers and risks his men would face in enemy skies. Time and again he refused to risk men's lives unless he was certain that the effort was in a good cause. He came close to turning down the Dambusters Raid, perhaps the most famous event in Lincolnshire's war, until convinced by Barnes Wallis that the bouncing bombs would actually work.

He was not, however, a particularly chatty or approachable man. He enjoyed his food and, even in 1939, was becoming rather portly as his job kept him increasingly tied to a desk. Indeed, he was known in Lincolnshire as 'Tubby' by the men he commanded and the name persisted here even when the newspapers came to call him 'Bomber'. Nor was Harris one to spend time visiting stations and bases on morale-boosting duties. He was firmly of the opinion that both he and his men had more important things to be getting on with. Despite this, or perhaps because of it, Harris proved to be popular with those serving under him. He trusted them to do their jobs, and they appreciated that trust.

There was a second man in 5 Group when war broke out who would later become one of the most skilled and famous squadron leaders of all time, though in September 1939 he was one pilot among many. This was Guy Gibson, flying with 83 Squadron. Like Harris, he was a gifted pilot and, again like Harris, he was a natural leader of men. While Harris toiled to get aircraft and equipment for his men to use on realistic targets, Gibson was working to improve bomb-aiming and air-gunnery at a squadron level. The partnership was one that was to last.

The organisation that Harris commanded, and in which Gibson served, was 5 Group of Bomber Command. In Lincolnshire, this Group consisted of eight squadrons at four airfields, and a Headquarters at Grantham. Hemswell was home to 61 and 144 Squadrons, Scampton to 49 and 83 Squadrons while 44 and 50 Squadrons were based at Waddington. Finally, 106 and 185 Squadrons were at Cottesmore.

In theory each squadron had 16 aircraft always ready for action, with enough spare aircraft, parts and crew on hand to cope with maintenance and sickness. In fact, none of the squadrons was at full strength when war came. Most would have been able to put up its full complement of 16 aircraft for a raid if given sufficient notice, but none was able to do so at short notice.

All the 5 Group squadrons were equipped with Handley Page Hampdens.

A pre-war publicity shot of the Hampden bomber with which 5 Group was equipped in 1939. The squared off glazed nose was replaced by a rounded nose in later models.

Harris was later to comment: 'The Hampden could do very little, but it did that very well indeed.' It was, in fact, one of the better bombers in service with the RAF when war broke out. It could fly higher, further and faster than other bombers and had a defensive armament of six 0.303 machine guns. The bomb load was disappointingly small for a twin-engined bomber, but it was able to carry the marine mines that Harris had sponsored at the Air Ministry.

The main drawback to the Hampden was its internal layout. All four members of the crew were cramped together in the front half of the fuselage, with the two gunners separated from the pilot and navigator/bomb-aimer by the bomb bay. There were, in effect, two crew compartments. At the front was a cabin for the pilot and navigator, who also acted as bomb-aimer and was usually a trained pilot himself. At the rear was a smaller cabin in which the dorsal gunner sat perched with his head poking out of the top of the fuselage, while the ventral gunner lay peering from the aircraft's belly.

The narrow fuselage made moving around in flight extremely difficult when wearing bulky flying gear so if the intercom failed, each man was effectively cut off from the rest. As with all British warplanes of this period the cockpit was open, though a perspex hood could be pulled over the pilot's head. The defensive guns were mounted on rails that supported the gun's weight while allowing the gunner to swing them around to face oncoming fighters – the idea of powered gun turrets was some years in the future.

Flying in one of these aircraft was a noisy, uncomfortable experience at the best of times. And at the service ceiling of almost 23,000 feet it was a very cold experience as well. Crew were cocooned in layers of warm clothing and wore thick gloves, which did nothing to improve their dexterity in action. A six-hour mission in such an aircraft was draining as the crew suffered from cold, vibration and constant noise. When the added stress of danger and enemy action was added, the flights of the Lincolnshire Hampdens became exhausting and terrifying.

It was with these aircraft that the men of Bomber Command in Lincolnshire went to war.

But if the men were well trained, well led and well equipped, they were handicapped by the orders they were given. Almost the first order Harris received was to stand down two of his squadrons to non-operational status. By October, 25% of the squadrons in 5 group had been cut. Harris chose

A Hampden bomber of 5 Group is loaded with a mine in 1940. Harris had supervised the development of air-dropped mines before the war and was a leading exponent of their use in the early months of conflict.

106 and 185. These two were to act as training squadrons and a reserve. Their primary role was to bring new crews up to operational standard, or to train existing crews in new skills or on new aircraft, while at the same time being on hand to undertake an important mission if all other squadrons were busy.

The second limiting move concerned targets. Bomber Command had assumed that the light bombers would support the army on the battlefield – and 1 Group with its single-engined Fairey Battles had already moved to France on 2 September – while it was thought the medium bombers such as the Hampdens would attack armaments factories, rail and road bridges and similar strategic targets. Now the Lincolnshire squadrons, and the rest of Bomber Command, were ordered not to attack any such targets.

The interior of a Whitley looking aft from the navigator's station towards the rear turret. The Whitley was one of the roomier bombers in service in 1940.

The Government had become painfully aware that the Luftwaffe had in excess of 1,200 front line bombers, compared to the 350 of the RAF and a similar number operated by France. It was feared that any attack that inflicted casualties on German civilians might provoke a massive response from the Luftwaffe. With these fears in mind, and urged on by an insistent French government, the British government banned Bomber Command from attacking any factory or transport link in a built up area. That effectively ruled out every factory in Germany and nearly every strategic bridge. Only warships at sea or anchored off the coast were deemed legitimate targets for attack.

Bomber Command was, however, allowed to raid deep into Germany so long as no bombs were dropped. These raids were given the codename 'Nickel' and had as their official objective the dropping of leaflets. These pieces of paper carried messages urging the German people to make peace and overthrow the Nazis. They had no effect whatsoever on a German public buoyed up by the annexation of Austria and Czechoslovakia and the swift conquest of Poland. Harris was, as usual, blunt: 'My personal view is that the only thing achieved is largely to supply the enemy's requirements of toilet paper.'

The missions were not, as it turned out, totally pointless. The crews took numerous photographs for reconnaissance purposes and tested their aircraft and equipment in combat conditions. The first thing that the crews reported back was that navigational maps and equipment were poor and of little use in finding a town, never mind a particular factory. Their second complaint was about the cold. Heating systems would clearly be required if long missions were to become normal routine. Word was sent to the aircraft factories, but it would be months before either situation was improved.

The main lesson that was learned, supported by information from squadrons in groups flying other missions, was that the British bombers were horribly vulnerable to German fighters. The bombers could fly at about 250 mph, while the Messerschmitt Bf109 could top 350 mph with ease. Moreover the 109 packed a powerful punch with two machine guns and two 20 mm cannon firing exploding shells that could, literally, tear a bomber to pieces. Just as deadly was the Messerschmitt Bf110, a twin-engined long-range fighter, that carried four machine guns and two cannon firing forward as well as a fifth machine gun that was operated independently by the navigator.

Working together, the two types of German fighter made a terrible double act, as 50 Squadron was to discover on an early daylight raid attacking German warships in the south-eastern waters of the North Sea. The Hampdens were flying at around 50 feet above the waves when they were noticed by a pair of long-range Messerschmitt 110s. A short while later three Messerschmitt 109s arrived, circling high overhead as the Messerschmitt 110s dived down to attack.

The German pilots had clearly discovered the Hampden's blind spot, a location just in front of and under the wing on which none of the defensive guns could be trained. One of the German Messerschmitt 110s approached the Hampden on the left of the British formation, edged into this position and opened fire with its navigator's gun. The British aircraft dived straight into the sea and vanished in a plume of spray. As the Messerschmitt 110 steered to repeat the trick on the next Hampden, the British pilot pulled his aircraft up and veered right to allow his gunners to reach the German. At once, the three 109s dived down and sprayed the Hampden with fire. The bomber exploded.

With no cloud in sight to offer cover and miles from land of any description, the men of 50 Squadron were helpless. No matter what they tried, the teamwork of the Germans proved deadly. Over the next ten minutes four

A German light flak gun. These weapons proved to be deadly against low-flying bombers operating in daylight during the early years of the war. (http://www.bomberhistory.co.uk)

*The interior of an air raid shelter on an RAF base in Lincolnshire.
Luftwaffe attacks were fortunately rare. (www.oldairfields.fotopic.net)*

more Hampdens were sent into the sea, killing all their crew. Only when running short of fuel did the Germans break off their murderous attacks.

When he got back to Waddington, Squadron Leader Watts filed an angry and detailed report that Harris ensured got on to the desk of Air Marshal Charles Portal MC DSO and bar, the head of Bomber Command, within 24 hours. When he read it, Portal promptly cancelled all future daylight operations unless a fighter escort could be provided.

Henceforth, the men of Bomber Command operating from Lincolnshire were to operate only at night. They would fly by night almost for the rest of the war.

On 2 May 1940, one such night mission to the Ruhr was undertaken by 144 Squadron. By this date the Germans had ringed their industrial cities with anti-aircraft guns and searchlights. One of these caught in its blinding beam was the Hampden in which Pilot Officer Robert Allitt was navigator and second pilot. At once the flak bursts began grouping around the aircraft. One close miss exploded only feet from the slender fuselage, just in front of the tail. The red hot shrapnel tore into the aircraft, slicing

19

Long disused, a toilet block stands forlornly at a former RAF base in the 5 Group area. (http://.oldairfields.fotopic.net/)

through the cables linking the pilot's controls to the tail. The plane swerved wildly and dived steeply. A second shell smashed an engine to ruins while a third sent splinters flying through the crew compartment. Nobody was seriously injured, but the fuselage was dotted with holes into which the freezing wind howled and much equipment was rendered useless.

Despite the damage, the pilot got the aircraft back under control. Left without lights or maps by the flak, Allitt fell back on his memory of where they were and his ability to navigate by the stars. Shouting instructions up through the narrow fuselage and over the howling wind, Allitt directed the pilot westward. Estimating that they had flown about 100 miles, Allitt told the pilot that he thought they were over France. Unable to land the damaged aircraft, the pilot gave the order to bale out. It was with great relief that the crew discovered Allitt had navigated them correctly. They gave themselves up to a French army patrol and in less than two days were back home at Hemswell.

A few nights later, a Hampden of 50 Squadron piloted by Squadron

Leader D.C. Good was one of several aircraft sent out to investigate reports of German troops and panzers massing on the western frontier as if preparing for an attack. When flying close to the Dutch border, Good's aircraft came under anti-aircraft fire. Reasoning that the Germans must be trying to protect something from prying eyes, Good put his Hampden into a turning dive that brought it down to barely 2,000 feet over an area of open countryside.

Navigator Walter Gardiner had just begun to distinguish what appeared to be trucks or panzers on the dark ground when the entire aircraft shuddered and was enveloped in a blinding flash of light. Smoke filled the cockpit in a choking cloud as the plane veered into a sideslip that was taking it dangerously close to the ground. Deafened by the blast of what they quickly realised had been an anti-aircraft shell bursting inside the fuselage, Good and Gardiner struggled to regain their senses.

As the smoke was blown back by the wind, Good managed to get the aircraft under control. Pushing the engines to full power, he pulled the nose up and was beginning to regain vital height when he suddenly passed out.

Only then did Gardiner realise that Good was injured, blood dripping from the torn shreds of his uniform. Calling to one of the gunners to crawl through the bomb bay to the front cabin to administer first aid to Good, Gardiner dragged the pilot from his seat and laid him on the floor. Gardiner scrambled into the empty pilot's seat just in time to get the Hampden climbing again as it had sunk into a gentle glide back towards the ground.

Piloting and navigating at the same time, helped by a map held up by the gunner, Gardiner managed to get the damaged aircraft back over the North Sea. Arriving over Waddington, Gardiner alerted base to the presence of a wounded man in a damaged aircraft, then performed a faultless landing. Both Good and Gardiner were awarded the Distinguished Flying Cross (DFC) for the night's action.

On 10 May Hitler unleashed his panzers in the terrifying blitzkrieg that took them across Belgium, Luxembourg and the Netherlands. The panzer spearheads punched a hole through the French lines at Sedan, crossing the Meuse and racing for the Channel before the Allies could reorganise to halt them. Cut off in northern France, the British Expeditionary Force was evacuated through Dunkirk. Although most of the men were brought safely home, they had left their equipment behind.

For Bomber Command, the savagery of the German attack led to a definitive change in orders and operations. On 14 May the Luftwaffe had bombed the Dutch city of Rotterdam to hasten the surrender of the Netherlands. Over 800 civilians were killed. Under threat of more massed air attacks, the Dutch government ordered its navy and air force to head for Britain, then surrendered.

The very next day the new British Prime Minister, Winston Churchill, summoned the head of Bomber Command to a cabinet meeting. Air Marshal Portal hurried across from the Air Ministry. He did not stay long. 'Take the gloves off,' said Churchill. Minutes later Portal was back at the Air Ministry phoning his Group Commanders with orders to attack factories and transport links in Germany itself with real bombs, not leaflets.

It was while Britain was still trying to digest the impact of the retreat from Dunkirk that 49 Squadron was sent out to attack a target in Germany. Acting Squadron Leader Robert Allen had barely got airborne from Scampton when he saw another aircraft looming up out of the night. Although the night was moonless and only starlight served to illuminate the scene, Allen recognised the bulbous nose and broad wings of a Heinkel III. Realising the enemy bomber had not seen him, Allen altered course to follow it.

The RAF built to last. These wartime workshops are now in use as farm buildings. (http://.oldairfields.fotopic.net/)

After several minutes of nerve-wracking tension, Allen managed to catch up with the German bomber. He brought his aircraft to within 20 yards of the enemy, at any moment expecting to be seen, then ordered his gunner, Sergeant Williams, to open fire. A stream of 200 bullets poured from the Hampden's dorsal gun and slammed into the Heinkel. For a moment, nothing seemed to happen. Then the German aircraft appeared to stagger slightly. Flames licked from one wing, gradually taking a hold all over the plane. Suddenly the Heinkel went nose down and plunged earthward, trailing a plume of flame through the darkness.

Allen then turned back on course for Germany to complete his original bombing mission. As if that were not enough for one night, Sergeant Williams later shot down a single-engined German aircraft over the target area. On their return, the crew were glad to discover that both Allen and Williams were put up for medals, with the pilot being given a DFC with great promptness.

It was meanwhile becoming rapidly apparent to the crews flying from Lincolnshire that one of their major problems was finding the target. The aircraft of a squadron took off within a few minutes of each other, then navigated independently to their allotted objective. A large proportion of crews reported themselves unable to locate their target, either through bad weather or simply by getting lost. Even those that did find the right town very often came under attack by anti-aircraft guns or were dazzled by searchlights and so were unable to locate the actual factory or dockyard they were meant to be destroying.

One Lincolnshire squadron accidentally found a solution to this problem, though it was not recognised as such at the time. In late May 49, Squadron was sent to bomb an armaments factory just outside Hamburg. Bomber crews found it easy to follow coastlines at night, as even faint starlight reflected off the water, so most of the aircraft got to Hamburg at the head of the Elbe estuary with ease. But they could not locate the factory.

Squadron Leader Geoffrey Lowe, however, did find the target. Shaking off a German fighter, Lowe dived in low and planted his bombs directly onto the factory. The blasts started a huge fire. By the light of this fire the other 15 aircraft of 49 Squadron that were flying about over Hamburg saw the target and bombed it both accurately and effectively.

A few weeks later a problem of a different kind was highlighted by 44 Squadron in a raid on Eschwege. Several of the aircraft came in low over the area in the hope of seeing the airfield that was their target for the night.

Inevitably these aircraft attracted the attentions of the searchlights and flak. One of these aircraft had as its bomb-aimer Pilot Officer David Romans. While scanning the ground for signs of an airfield, Romans became aware that the aircraft was dodging and diving in a most unusual manner. He tried to call the pilot on the intercom, but received no reply.

Clambering through the notoriously narrow fuselage of the Hampden, Romans got to the pilot's cockpit only to find the windshield blown away by an explosion and the pilot lolling senseless. The buckle securing the

Almost hidden in undergrowth, the concrete escape hatch from a wartime shelter pokes above the ground at a now derelict RAF base in Lincolnshire.
(http://.oldairfields.fotopic.net/)

pilot in his seat would not come undone, so Romans was unable to pull him clear. Instead he had to climb up to sit on the pilot's lap and grab the control column. This put Romans in a position where he could not reach the rudder pedals and with his head sticking up into the bitterly cold slipstream of the night air over Germany.

Romans had been keeping the aircraft in the air for some 20 minutes in this fashion when one of the gunners crawled over the bomb bay to reach the cockpit to find out what was going on. He was able to cut the pilot free, allowing Romans finally to get into the seat. While the gunner patched up the wounded pilot, probably saving his life, Romans brought the aircraft back to England and a rather bumpy landing.

Clearly the habit of coming in low to locate the target accurately was a hazardous procedure. The problems of navigation and bomb-aiming at night would continue to bedevil RAF missions for many months. The concept of target marking, as fortuitously achieved by Squadron Leader Lowe, would not be undertaken deliberately until much later in the war. Though when it was begun, it would yield massive results.

Thus the strategic bomber offensive on Germany began. It would be five years, almost to the day, before it ended.

Handley Page Hampden

Type:	Medium bomber
Engines:	Mk I 2 x 980 hp
	Bristol Pegasus XVIII
	Mk II (Hereford) 2 x
	1,000 hp Napier Dagger VIII
Wingspan:	69 ft 2 in
Length:	53 ft 7 in
Height:	14 ft 11 in
Weight:	Empty 11,780 lb
	Loaded 21,000 lb
Armament:	6 x 0.303 in machine guns in nose turret, dorsal and
	ventral positions
Bombload:	4,000 lb of bombs, or one mine or one torpedo
Max speed:	265 mph
Ceiling:	22,700 ft
Range:	1,200 miles
Production:	1,532

The Hampden was a standard bomber for the RAF on the outbreak of war, and all the squadrons in Lincolnshire were equipped with this aircraft. It was the first monoplane bomber to be produced by the Handley Page company and the prototype flew in June 1936. Although it was not able to carry as heavy a bomb load as the government specification had stated, the Hampden was fast and able to fly at high altitude. It was soon found to be vulnerable to German fighters, while its restricted bomb load made it of only limited use against strategic targets in Germany. By late in 1941 it was being phased out of use by Bomber Command, although Coastal Command kept it in service as a long-range mine layer and torpedo bomber until 1944. A batch of 100 Hampdens equipped with the more powerful Napier engines were being built for Sweden in 1939, but when war broke out they were commandeered for use as a trainer and dubbed 'Hereford'.

Chapter 2

Lincolnshire
Hits Back

The collapse of France and the Battle of Britain that followed brought profound changes to Bomber Command in Lincolnshire. As ever, the men serving in the county were ready for the challenge and proved able to meet it.

First to be affected was the popular commander of 5 Group, Arthur Harris. His efficiency and hard work had been noticed by Charles Portal, head of Bomber Command. When Portal was promoted to Chief of the Air Staff he asked Harris to join him as his deputy with special responsibility for supervising the design and production of bombers. Harris left Lincolnshire with a heavy heart, but kept in contact with many of his men and watched their progress with interest. It was

The statue of Charles Portal that stands outside the Ministry of Defence in London.

noticeable that in later years, whenever Harris needed a man for a difficult assignment, he turned first to men who had served under him in Lincolnshire.

Harris stayed at the Air Ministry for only a few months before going to America to advise the aircraft industry there on the demands of modern air warfare. His time in London was significant for one incident more than any other. One night in December, Portal summoned Harris and other officers to the rooftop walk of the Air Ministry in Westminster. The City of London and the East End were being pounded by hundreds of Luftwaffe bombers dropping high explosives and incendiaries. The ancient churches and modern office buildings went up in flames as London's firemen struggled to control the all enveloping conflagration. The sky was red with flames towering hundreds of feet into the air.

A pre-war illustration of Fairey Battles, the aircraft with which 1 Group squadrons were equipped when they first arrived in Lincolnshire. The artist has rather optimistically shown the aircraft performing a practice dive-bombing manoeuvre over the English countryside. The Battles were unsuited to dive-bombing.

Portal noticed that Harris alone was silent, glaring at the terrible sight laid out in front of the assembled senior officers.

'What do you think?' asked Portal.

Harris kept his eyes fixed on the burning city as he answered. 'They are sowing the wind,' he said evenly. Harris left unsaid the rest of the Biblical quotation from the Book of Hosea, an Old Testament prophet: 'For they have sown the wind, and they shall reap the whirlwind.'

Today a fine statue of Portal stands outside the Ministry of Defence in London. It shows him as so many of his close colleagues remember him, with his head lifted to stare at the skies to the south-east – the direction from which the German bombers came during the Blitz.

Meanwhile the men of Bomber Command in Lincolnshire continued with the job in hand. The squadrons of 5 Group were joined by those of 1 Group. Ten squadrons of Bomber Command had been sent out to France in September 1939 to act as a battlefield support group to the

A newspaper advert from Vickers published in 1940 emphasises the contribution of the company to the RAF. Note the Wellington bomber has had its armament obscured for security reasons.

British Expeditionary Force, being officially known as the Advanced Air Striking Force. They were all equipped with the Fairey Battle, which proved spectacularly ineffective in combat. The Battle was a single-engined, two seater able to carry two 500 lb bombs. In theory the Battles were supposed to launch short-range raids on enemy troops and supply columns. In practice those that were hurled forward against the advancing German armies in May and June 1940 were outclassed by the German fighters. The squadrons suffered appalling casualties – one raid of 71 Battles attacking the bridges over the Meuse River at Sedan lost no fewer than 41 aircraft.

The battered survivors of 1 Group were brought back to England. They thankfully gave up their Battles in favour of the far superior Vickers Wellington and were sent to new stations. Squadrons 12 and 103 came to Lincolnshire to form the basis of a new 1 Group. It was 103 Squadron that got into action first. Posted to Elsham Wolds airfield in July 1940 they arrived to find that their new base had no water, no electricity, no runway and no control tower. Even the accommodation blocks were only half built.

The crest used by 9 Squadron, one of the bomber squadrons that was decimated over France in 1940, then brought back to Lincolnshire to be rebuilt and to form the basis of 1 Group.

Despite these problems, the squadron flew its first mission just three days after arriving, sending six Wellingtons to attack Bremen. One aircraft, piloted by Pilot Officer Kenneth Wallis, suffered severe icing while it was over the target and had one engine cut out. Dropping down to a lower altitude to get rid of the ice, Wallis crossed the English coast at Harwich. There his aircraft came under sustained fire from the anti-aircraft batteries, the gunners mistaking the Wellington for a Heinkel. Dodging desperately to avoid the gunfire, the Wellington hit a balloon cable which sliced deep into the wing. Despite all this, Wallis got his aircraft back to Elsham Wolds, though the undercarriage collapsed on landing and the plane was a write-off.

This flight, and many others like it, demonstrated the rugged construction of the Wellington and explained its popularity with crews. There was a strong feeling among the men who flew these

The interior of a Wellington looking aft from the navigator's station towards the rear turret. The Wellington was one of the roomier bombers in service in 1940. (http://www.oldairfields.fotopic.net/)

machines that the Wellington would get them home if it possibly could. Even much later in the war when newer and more powerful aircraft became available, many crews preferred the steady 'Wimpey' as they called it in deference to a newspaper cartoon character of the time.

The men of 5 Group were still flying their Hampdens, and would continue to do so until December 1941. Like the squadrons of the forming 1 Group, 5 Group was being sent to attack targets in Germany. The aircraft of 2 Group and 3 Group, based mostly in East Anglia, were busy bombing the armies that Hitler was gathering in northern France and the Low Countries for the invasion of Britain. With their longer range and heavier bomb load, the men of Lincolnshire were sent after more strategic targets. Aircraft factories were listed as being the top priority, followed by transport links, oil refineries and other armaments works. In the long summer evenings, the crews sought to take advantage of the dwindling light to find their targets, then return home under cover of darkness.

It was on one such flight that Flying Officer Geoffrey Hall of 61 Squadron had an early brush with what would become one of the greatest dangers facing the men of Bomber Command. Hall was part of a force sent to attack a munitions factory at Aachen. As he approached the target, Hall found himself caught in a searchlight beam. Soon three more searchlights homed in on the Hampden and held it despite Hall's attempts to shake them off.

Navigators from a bomber squadron 'somewhere in England' study their maps prior to a raid, July 1940. At this date finding a target was a rather hit or miss affair.

Much to his surprise, Hall did not become the target for the anti-aircraft guns that had previously invariably followed the searchlights. He soon discovered why. A Messerschmitt 109 fighter came diving down on the rear of the Hampden, opening fire at devastatingly close range. The upper rear gunner replied with great skill, seeing his bullets strike the wing of the German plane, which then dived away out of sight. The Hampden was also damaged, having taken hits in both wings, the central fuselage and the tail plane, which was hanging almost in shreds.

Despite the damage, Hall pushed on to the target, dropping his bombs before turning for home. He had had a lucky escape. At this date the German fighter pilots were still learning the difficult skills of aerial warfare at night. They relied upon searchlights to find their prey and even then were often wary of pushing an attack home. The situation would soon change as the pilots gained the skills and the equipment needed for effective night fighting.

At about the same time Pilot Officer Charles Price of 44 Squadron took a very different attitude to night-fighters. Returning from a raid on an aircraft

A photo taken during a raid on Rotterdam in July 1940. Such low-level daylight raids proved to be very costly and were soon abandoned.

Bomber crews walk past a hangar 'somewhere in England', July 1940. Their dress shows they are preparing for a mission.

factory at Bremen in July, Price was passing the Luftwaffe base of Borkum at a height of 500 feet. He spotted three Messerschmitt 110 fighters above the airfield. Realising that he had not been seen by the German pilots, Price manoeuvred his aircraft so that he was approaching them from behind and below. This move put his Hampden in the only blind spot on the otherwise highly effective Messerschmitt 110.

Alerting his gunners to what he was doing over the intercom, Price got right beneath the Germans. The British gunners then opened fire at almost point blank range. One German aircraft turned on its back with fire pouring

33

Schipol Airport in Holland was commandeered by the Luftwaffe in 1940. It is shown here as photographed by an attacking RAF bomber. 1 Runways; 2 Bomb bursts; 3 German aircraft; 4 Damaged aircraft.

from the port engine and dived vertically into the sea. A second was hit repeatedly and dived down out of sight, while the third fled the scene at high speed. Such success against night-fighters was rare, and would soon become almost impossible.

Difficulties of another kind were encountered by 44 Squadron when attacking an aircraft factory at Dessan in the first week of August. Arriving over the target, the pilots found that the factory layout below them bore no resemblance at all to the briefing they had been given before take off. Clearly the Germans had been building new workshops since the intelligence photos had been taken, or the photos had been of some other factory.

Rather than scatter his bombs and hope for a hit, Pilot Officer Charles

The cover of the instruction booklet issued to all pilots flying Wellington bombers during the war. Similar booklets were supplied to each member of the crew, giving detailed instructions on the controls they would use and their duties in flight. Other aircraft had similar booklets for crew members. Overleaf: views of the pilot's controls.

Hattersley went in on a reconnaisance pass that took him low over the factory. Despite coming under machine gun fire, Hattersley made a second pass before managing to locate a large building which had high tension electricity cables running from it to other buildings. Reasoning that this must house the main electricity generator of the complex, Hattersley returned for a third pass, this time dropping his bombs with accuracy on the generator building, which was utterly destroyed. His report highlighted the need for accurate intelligence if any raid was to be a success.

On 12 August 49 Squadron was ordered to attack one of the most important transport links in Germany. This was the aqueduct that carried the Dortmund-Ems Canal over a valley north of Munster. Vast quantities of German industrial goods travelled along this canal, and the aqueduct was the only spot where it was vulnerable to bombs. Six Hampdens from 49 Squadron took off, joined by another five from 83 Squadron. Among the pilots flying from Scampton with 49 Squadron was Roderick Learoyd, a 27-year-old native of Kent who had joined the RAF in 1936.

Learoyd's was detailed to be the fifth and final aircraft to attack the narrow aqueduct. At just past 11 pm Learoyd arrived over the Ems River, a short distance north of the target. The scene below was bathed in the clear blue light of a cloudless half moon. Learoyd had no trouble picking out the silver ribbon of the river, nor the spot where it was crossed by the canal.

Suddenly the peaceful scene erupted into flame and fire. Squadron Leader James Pitcairn-Hill was making his bombing run, the first of the night, and the German defences were throwing shell and bullets up into the sky. Pitcairn-Hill scored a narrow miss, so a second bomber, piloted by Australian Pilot Officer Edward Ross, moved into the attack. A searchlight found the bomber as it lined up for the bombing run. Flak shells quickly followed, blasting the bomber to pieces. There were no survivors.

The third bomber to enter the maelstrom of gunfire was piloted by another Australian, A.R. Mulligan. It too was caught by a searchlight

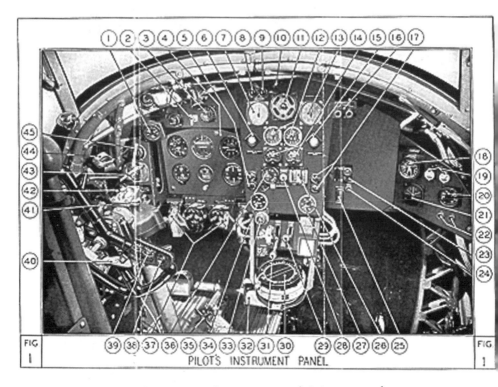

1 Bomb steering indicator 2 Bomb jettison control 3 Auto-controls pressure gauge
4 Instrument flying panel 5 Starter and booster coil pushbuttons – port engine
6 Propeller feathering switch – port engine 7 Port engine speed indicator
8 Undercarriage warning horn test pushbutton 9 Fuel contents gauges pushbutton
10 Windscreen wiper controls 11 Undercarriage indicator 12 Boost gauges (two)
13 Starboard engine speed indicator 14 Cylinder temperature gauges (two)
15 Propeller feathering switch – starboard engine 16 Oil tank low-level warning
lights (two) 17 Starter and booster coil pushbuttons – starboard engine
18 Pneumatic pressure gauge 19 Fire extinguisher pushbuttons (two)
20 Air temperature gauge 21 DF indicator 22 Fuel pressure warning lights (two)
23 Pilot's call light 24 Flare launching warning light 25 Suction gauge
26 Oil pressure gauge (two) 27 Oil temperature gauge – starboard engine
28 Boost gauge reversal control 29 Flap control lever 30 Compass
31 Undercarriage selector lever 32 Rudder pedal – starboard 33 Windscreen de-icing
pump 34 Oil temperature gauge – port engine 35 Rudder bar adjustment wheel
36 Flap indicator 37 Cowling gill controls (two) 38 Intercom microphone
pushbutton 39 Torpedo release pushbuttons (two) 40 Brake lever 41 Brake locking
slide 42 Bomb release pushbutton 43 Bomb doors control 44 Landing lamps switch
45 Bomb master switch

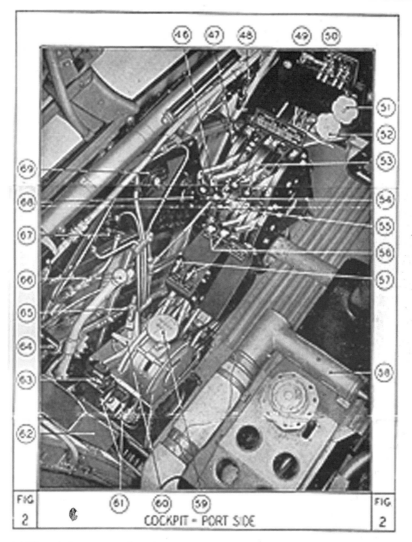

FIG 2 — COCKPIT - PORT SIDE — FIG 2

46 Throttle levers 47 Throttle levers' friction adjuster 48 TR9 remote control
49 Undercarriage indicator switch 50 Ignition switches 51 Fuel jettisoning air valve
control 52 Fuel jettisoning valve control 53 Mixture control levers 54 Supercharger
control 55 Carburettor air intake control 56 Propellor speed controls
57 Slow running cut out controls 58 Pilot's heating diffuser 59 Elevator and rudder
trimming tab control 60 Elevator trimming tab fine adjustment control 61 Engine
master cock controls (two) 62 Map stowage 63 Fuel pressure balance cock (A)
control 64 Micro/telephone socket 65 Aileron (port only) trimming tab control
66 Landing lamp lowering lever 67 Autopilot control cock 68 Autopilot steering
lever 69 Autopilot attitude control

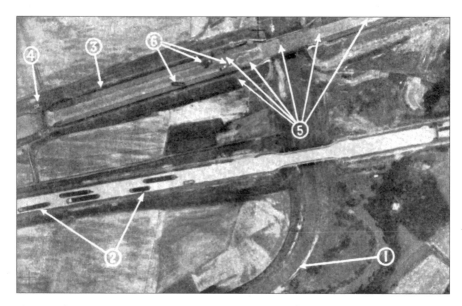

Publicity photos released by the Air Ministry reveal the damage done to the
Dortmund-Ems Canal in the raid in which Roderick Learoyd won a VC. Above:
The canal before the raid showing (at the top of the picture) the unfinished new
viaduct and (at the bottom of the picture) the original viaduct carrying canal barges.
Below: A photo taken after the raid. The original key reads: 2 Canal out of
operation, water seeping through the gates at 3 and new dam built at 4 to stop flow
of water; 5 bomb craters; 6 Old aqueduct, a large part broken away by bombing,
repair work in progress.

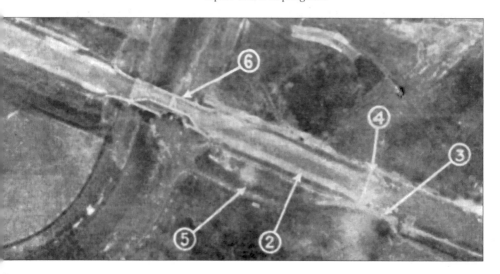

and hit by anti-aircraft guns. Mulligan jettisoned his bombs, then climbed rapidly into the protective darkness. Within seconds it became clear the aircraft would not make the long journey back to Lincolnshire, so the crew bailed out to spend the rest of the war in captivity. While in prison camp in Germany, Mulligan was to learn that he had been awarded a DFC for his night's work. The fourth attack was made by Pilot Officer Matthews, who hit one end of the aqueduct, causing some damage but not enough to put the canal out of action.

Finally, it was Learoyd's turn to attack. By this time the defences were not only fully awake, but had found the height of the attacking aircraft. Searchlight beams weaved around the sky seeking out new victims for the guns. Undeterred by having already seen two of his fellow bombers go down, Learoyd began his attack.

Unlike the other aircraft, which had dived on the target, Learoyd dropped down to just 150 feet above the ground while more than 3 miles away. He then flew along the canal, having ordered his two gunners to fire at the searchlights as they approached the target. The bomb-aimer, Lewis, got into the nose of the aircraft ready to release his deadly cargo. Hurtling along at over 200 mph, the Hampden was rapidly approaching the aqueduct when the Germans heard it coming from the darkness. It took a searchlight only seconds to find the bomber, after which the machine guns opened up. Learoyd's gunners returned the fire, filling the night air with the sounds of gunfire to add to the roaring of the engines.

Suddenly the bomber lurched to the left. Learoyd struggled to get the aircraft back on course, but had great difficulty. Moments later Lewis shouted 'OK' and the aircraft jumped upward as the weight of the bombs fell clear of the bomb bay. Learoyd hauled the control column back and to his right, causing the aircraft to soar into the darkness away from the searchlights and flak guns. Far beneath, his bombs tore the aqueduct to pieces, putting the canal out of action for some weeks.

Once clear of the immediate danger, Learoyd could assess the damage to his aircraft. The terrific blow felt as they came into attack turned out to have been caused by an anti-aircraft shell that had smashed clean through the starboard wing, miraculously without exploding. The shell left a gaping hole, but had managed to miss both the main supporting strut and the fuel tank. A bullet or shell splinter had pierced the main hydraulic tank, so the landing gear would not work and the wing flaps were useless.

Learoyd opted to make for home. He reached Scampton just before dawn, then circled, waiting for daylight to come and give him a better chance of landing intact. Lewis cranked the landing gear down by hand, allowing Learoyd to put his battered aircraft down safely.

Just eight days later, Learoyd was awarded a Victoria Cross for his attack. The citation mentioned not just his great heroism in making a successful attack in the face of great danger, but also the flying skill and determination he had displayed on many previous occasions.

Unlike far too many of the heroes of Bomber Command, Learoyd survived to enjoy his rewards. He rose to be commander of his squadron, then was transferred to an Operational Training Unit (OTU) to train new crews in combat tactics. In 1942 he took command of 44 Squadron for a second tour of operations, then was returned to training duties before moving to the Air Ministry. During the war the length of a 'tour' that an airman was expected to complete before a spell away from combat duties varied greatly. In the early months of war it was entirely up to the airman and his squadron commander, with the occasional intervention of the medical officer, when a rest was needed. Later in the war a tour was standardised as being composed of 30 operations over enemy territory, with other missions such as diversionary raids or mine-laying scoring as half a mission for the purpose of calculating a tour's duration. After the war Learoyd went back to his peacetime career in the motorcar industry.

Learoyd's was the first Victoria Cross to be won by the men of Bomber Command in Lincolnshire, but it was far from the last.

August was a busy month for 83 Squadron at Scampton, and no one was busier than Acting Squadron Leader John Collier. One night he was detailed to lead a hazardous diversionary raid while the rest of the bomber force attacked factories in the Ruhr. Collier's task was to hit a target in northern Germany timed for half an hour before the main attack went in. Having diverted German attention, Collier was to fly home. The raid proved to be only too successful. Flying in off the sea at very low level – Collier estimated he was at around 200 feet – the Hampden drew the attention of every German in the area. Dropping his bombs, Collier turned for home. When he landed, Collier and his crew found their Hampden riddled with bullet holes. The aircraft was taken for repair.

Despite this close escape, Collier took off in a new aircraft the very next night to lead a main attack on an oil refinery and storage depot near Dortmund. He arrived over Dortmund soon after midnight and, after some difficulty, identified the target. Again he chose to attack at low level, this time going down to barely 100 feet as he approached the huge storage tanks. At such a low height, Collier could not miss. His bombs plunged into a vast, drum-shaped tank. An ear-splitting roar filled the air as the tank exploded in a sheet of flame that leapt high into the sky. The blast hit the bomber as if some invisible giant had kicked the rear of the aircraft with a gigantic boot. Struggling to gain control, Collier circled up into the air to get a view of the destruction below. As he stared down, a second tank exploded in a blinding flash, so Collier decided it was wise to leave the area. Once again, his aircraft was riddled with bullet holes.

For the double attack, Collier was awarded a DFC, to which he was to win a bar in September 1941 by which time he was with 44 Squadron.

Another attack that month brought a DFC to 61 Squadron. The raid was against warships in Wilhelmshaven. Bad weather meant that only one aircraft, that piloted by Pilot Officer Dudley Davis, managed to locate the port. Despite finding his aircraft alone, Davis dived down to attacking height and headed for the docks. Every anti-aircraft gun in the town poured its fire at the lone Hampden, but it somehow escaped serious damage and dropped its bombs into the harbour. Unable to see if he had hit anything important, Davis raced away at a dangerously low height before climbing and turning for home.

By late August, a German invasion of Britain seemed imminent. Panzer divisions were massed in northern France and German reconnaissance aircraft were busily photographing landing beaches and routes inland. The squadrons based in Lincolnshire were taken off strategic targets in Germany and instead directed to attack the ships being gathered to transport the German army to Britain.

One of the largest concentrations of Rhine barges and transport aircraft was gathering in Antwerp, where the bases were protected by a dense ring of German anti-aircraft guns, barrage balloons and searchlights. On 15 September 83 Squadron at Scampton was given orders to attack Antwerp and the ships moored there.

Among the airmen to take part in the raid was Sergeant John Hannah. Aged just 18, Hannah was already a veteran of several operational raids across the North Sea, flying in Hampdens with three equally experienced colleagues: Pilot Officer Connor, Sergeant Hayhurst and Sergeant James.

The raid was at first successful. Hayhurst guided the aircraft accurately to Antwerp, and Connor saw the dark silhouettes of his targets outlined against the water of the harbour. Unfortunately there was a strong crosswind, which caused the aircraft to drift off course as it made its bombing run. The second run was more successful and the bombs were dropped on target. Suddenly a deafening explosion rocked the aircraft, lifting the Hampden bodily upwards. A German shell had exploded just beneath the left wing root, causing extensive damage to the bomb bay area and puncturing the wing with shrapnel. Fuel poured from the wing, struck the hot engine and burst into flames.

Sergeant James, close to the damage, was at once faced by a wall of flames and lost no time in baling out. Deeper in the fuselage, Hannah did not think the fire was too serious. Connor asked Hannah to take a closer look, but when he could not open the door to the bomb bay area, Connor sent Hayhurst to check things out. The small 24-inch door from the pilot's compartment to the bomb bay area was stuck. When Hayhurst succeeded in kicking the door open, he was faced by a scene of such devastation that he believed the aircraft was doomed. Like James, he baled out.

Hannah, meanwhile, had managed to get his door to the bomb bay area open and entered the central compartment. He grabbed a fire extinguisher and went to work on the flames. The first extinguisher ran out, so he emptied the second on the dwindling blaze. The second extinguisher failed to complete the job, so Hannah used his log book and then his hands to beat out the remnants of the fire. By this stage, his hands and arms were badly burned, but Hannah refused to bale out and instead scrambled painfully through the hatch into the pilot's compartment.

Once in position, he and Connor decided to try to fly the aircraft back to Scampton. Hannah tried to make sense of Hayhurst's charts and gave Connor a bearing to follow. The bearing proved to be inaccurate, but fortunately Hannah recognised landmarks as he crossed the Lincolnshire coast and managed to guide Connor to Scampton by sight.

The badly damaged Hampden came down safely and ambulance crews raced to get the two survivors to hospital. Hannah was awarded a Victoria Cross for his actions that night, while Connor received a DFC. Sadly, neither man was to enjoy his medal for long. Connor was killed on a mission a few weeks later, while Hannah never fully recovered from the burns and smoke inhalation he had suffered. He died of tuberculosis on 7 June 1947. Today, Hannah's VC is on display at the RAF Museum in Hendon while his grave is at Markham Cemetery, Leicester.

During the same raid in which Hannah earned his VC, a pilot from 44 Squadron was winning his DFC. Arriving as one of the first aircraft to reach Antwerp, Pilot Officer Wilfred Lewis opted to use his Hampden as a dive-bomber. He hoped to be able to approach at altitude, evading searchlights and so take the anti-aircraft gunners by surprise. The plan did not work out as planned.

Lewis got into position to start his dive without being seen, but was caught by a searchlight almost as soon as he began his descent. Raked by machine gun fire, the aircraft veered wildly out of control. The bomb-aimer caught a sudden glimpse of the target barges passing into view as the Hampden careered across the sky and let go the bombs. Relieved of the weight, the bomber suddenly righted itself and Lewis was able to regain control. Although he was forced to fight the controls all the way, Lewis piloted the damaged aircraft back to Waddington safely.

Some indication of the stress the men of Bomber Command in Lincolnshire were under at this time can be gained by the fact that Lewis's citation when being awarded his medal recorded that this was his thirty-eighth mission over enemy territory in less than six months. Such a record was not unusual among the men flying from Lincolnshire.

It wasn't just military targets that attracted bombers from Lincolnshire at this time. The Germans had commandeered all supplies of fuel in France in preparation for the invasion of Britain. The Hampdens of 61 Squadron were sent out to attack a large oil depot at Bordeaux. As usual at this date, the aircraft made their way individually to the target. Given the long range of this attack, the outbound journey gave plenty of opportunity for aircraft to get lost or fall behind the others.

The Hampden flown by Pilot Officer Peter De Mestre arrived over Bordeaux to find a peaceful and tranquil scene. Thinking that he must be the first to arrive, De Mestre circled slowly to identify the depot, then dived down to attack. Unfortunately for De Mestre he was actually the last of the aircraft to arrive and the German defenders were ready and waiting for him. At 2,000 feet, the Hampden was struck by the glare of a searchlight, which soon brought in its trail a withering fire from anti-aircraft guns. One shell burst alongside the fuselage, smashing the aircraft's radio and several flying instruments. Moments later a second shell exploded just in front of the port wing, peppering the engine with shrapnel. Despite the damage, De Mestre completed the bombing run and planted his bombs into the depot.

Once clear of the target, the crew surveyed the damage to their aircraft. They decided to head for home, rather than make the shorter flight to Spain where they would be interned. While heading north over France,

De Mestre was shocked to find his damaged engine suddenly cutting out. As they flew over Normandy the one remaining engine began to splutter and cough. Over the English Channel this engine also failed. With great skill, De Mestre managed to glide his aircraft to a deserted beach where he performed a crash-landing.

Uninjured, the crew scrambled out of the wreck. They were at once pounced on by a Home Guard unit concerned they might be German agents reconnoitring a possible invasion landing point. Hurried explanations followed and the airmen were back at base the next day.

Also in September, a flight of 44 Squadron were sent to attack the hundreds of barges gathered in Ostend harbour. Acting Squadron Leader William Gardner was first to arrive over the target. A strict blackout meant the harbour was in darkness, while the lack of moonlight meant that it was difficult to identify anything worth bombing.

While the other aircraft circled overhead, Gardner went down to 800 feet to survey the scene. An intense and accurate anti-aircraft fire came up, badly damaging the Hampden. Gardner had, however, found what he

A reconnaissance photo taken after a raid on Ostend. As can be seen, most of the dockside warehouses now stand roofless.

was looking for. Turning back on his course, Gardner made another run over the port, bombing the barges with such accuracy that each of his eight bombs was seen to strike and sink a different vessel. The other bombers then came in to attack with an accuracy scarcely less impressive.

One of the following bombers was piloted by Wing Commander David Reid. By the time Reid came in on his bombing run the German gunners were throwing everything possible into the air. At a height of 500 feet, Reid's aircraft was struck by a stream of tracer and machine gun bullets that tore up through the floor of the cockpit. Most machine guns being fired at night included a number of tracer bullets in the belt of ammunition. These glowed white hot when fired and enabled the gunner to watch where he was shooting. They sometimes had the incidental advantage of setting fire to a target. Reid flinched as the canopy above him shattered into fragments and bullets lanced all around him. Seconds later the gunfire stopped. Reid was amazed to find that he was completely uninjured, although every single instrument in the cockpit had been hit and was out of action. Flying with the control column alone, Reid brought his aircraft home.

Although Churchill had ordered Portal to take off the gloves, the old policy of leaflet dropping had not been abandoned entirely. The RAF had given up on trying to persuade the German public to overthrow Hitler, but it was felt that keeping in touch with the occupied peoples of Europe was essential. Compact newsletters were printed giving the latest war news and dropped over those areas occupied by the Germans so that some people at least could get information unbiased by the Nazi propaganda machine.

In November, 49 Squadron was chosen for the task of scattering such leaflets. The aircraft navigated by Flying Officer George Reid was given Danzig (Gdansk) as a target. Reaching Poland would involve a flight of some five hours, followed by an equally long flight home. It was felt that such a long stretch over Germany itself was impossibly dangerous, so the coastal city of Danzig was chosen. Reid would thus be able to fly across sea for most of his time in the air and hopefully avoid enemy aircraft or gunfire.

In the event, Reid managed to navigate his aircraft across the North Sea and over Denmark with ease. Using a compass and taking bearings from the stars, he flew across the Baltic entirely out of sight of land, before turning south and making landfall directly over central Danzig. The leaflets were fed down the chutes designed to launch flares, and the aircraft turned for home. Again, Reid navigated out of sight of land for hours on end and

Bombs explode on the docks of Cherbourg during an RAF raid. French ports were targeted to stop their use by German forces.

arrived over Scampton spot on target. The aircraft was, however, almost out of fuel due to encountering a headwind on the return journey. As a result few leaflet raids followed against distant Poland, though France, Denmark, Norway and the Low Countries continued to receive such newsletters throughout the war.

The spring of 1941 revealed that Hitler had called off any thoughts of invading Britain, for that year at least. The vast panzer concentrations in northern France had gone, as had the gatherings of invasion shipping. In June 1941 Hitler launched his mighty armed forces against Russia, starting a war that would last for years and cause the deaths of millions. The respite this gave the British was short lived. The German navy had been ordered to starve Britain into surrender by sinking the merchant ships that carried food to the country. The Royal Navy fought a gruelling campaign against the U-boats and warships that struck at the merchant convoys. Although the Navy was ably assisted by RAF Coastal Command, it was sometimes necessary to call on Bomber Command as well.

Thus it was that Pilot Officer James Anderson of 103 Squadron found himself ordered to attack the dock facilities at Brest, in France, which were being used by the German navy. Taking off from Elsham Wolds on a clear June evening, Anderson was disappointed to find that the weather had closed in by the time he reached Brest. Dense low cloud or mist covered the town. After circling for over half an hour, despite the risk that night-fighters might be approaching, Anderson saw the low cloud part to reveal the docks.

Putting his Wellington into a gentle dive, Anderson descended to 900 feet before levelling out. As he approached the town, a massed battery of searchlights flicked on. The front gunner began firing, putting out first one then a second searchlight. A third light then caught the bomber, almost blinding Anderson with its glaring intensity. The gunner put that light out too, but then a fourth light found the Wellington, leading several more to 'cone' the bomber.

Despite incoming fire from heavy machine guns and light flak guns, Anderson managed to hold his aircraft steady. The bombs were dropped with pinpoint accuracy demolishing several dock buildings. As the Wellington raced away, the rear gunner put out several more searchlights with his twin machine guns. Tearing across the landscape at high speed, Anderson made good his escape. The Wellington was riddled with bullets, but returned safely to base. Once again, the attack had shown that only a low-level attack could achieve accuracy of bombing, but that such an attack was almost suicidally dangerous against prepared defences.

The following month, 106 Squadron and other units were sent back to Brest after a scout aircraft discovered the powerful warships *Gneisenau* and *Scharnhorst* in the port. These two warships, each armed with nine 11 inch and twelve 6 inch guns, had long been a serious problem to the Royal Navy. In 1940 they had led the German invasion of Norway, sinking a British aircraft carrier and two destroyers with ease. In February 1941 the two ships attacked an Atlantic convoy, sinking 22 ships in less than an hour. Their destruction was a top priority and, despite misgivings, 106 Squadron was ordered to attack in daylight to maximise the chances of accurate bombing.

Flying far out to sea and at almost wave-top height, the bombing force managed to reach Brest without being located by the Germans. Without waiting to get into formation or to reconnoitre the port, the bombers flew in to take full advantage of the element of surprise. The advantage did not last long for soon a heavy and concentrated anti-aircraft fire was coming up from the ships and from batteries along the dockside.

Pilot Officer James Erly of 106 Squadron scored a direct hit on the *Gneisenau*, which, combined with damage inflicted by other aircraft, put the battlecruiser out of action for several months. Along with Gordon Lane, Arthur Roberts and Max Roy of 103 Squadron, Erly was given a DFC for his exploits – just four of the 51 medals won during this action.

The raid was over in minutes, and the bombers turned for home. Soon Luftwaffe fighters intercepted the British formations and desperate combats led to several bombers being shot down. Fortunately a strong fighter force of Spitfires and Hurricanes was flying out from England to meet the raiders on their way home and was able to drive off the Messerschmitts before further carnage ensued. Only precise navigation and impeccable timing by both bombers and fighters had made the mission a success.

Throughout these months it was clear that bomber crews were still

A high-level reconnaissance photo taken by a Spitfire immediately prior to the famous bomber raid on the French port of Brest and released to the press soon afterwards. The original key reads: 1 The battle cruisers sewn to the quays by camouflage netting; 2 Camouflaged buildings; 3 Anti-torpedo boom; 4 Demolished oil tanks.

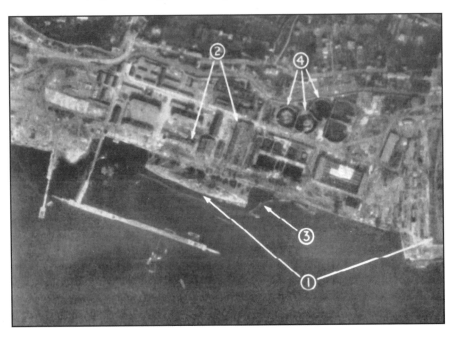

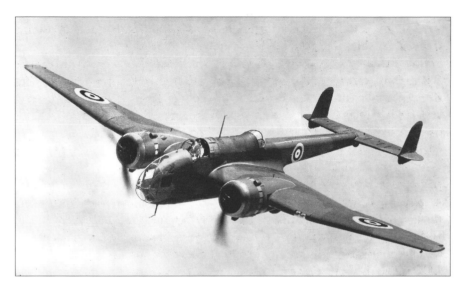

A late model Hampden in flight. After the Hampden was replaced on bombing missions by more modern aircraft it was fitted with extra fuel tanks and assigned to long-range maritime reconnaissance missions.

having difficulty both finding their targets and hitting them. Everyone in Lincolnshire was aware of the problems, but nobody appreciated quite how bad they were. Not until a detailed investigation was undertaken was it realised that barely 5% of bombs hit their targets. At the same time, German night-fighters were appearing in the skies over the Reich. Casualties among bomber crews began to rise alarmingly.

High casualties combined with poor results was no basis for a victorious campaign. Something would have to be done. The men of Bomber Command in Lincolnshire were facing a crisis.

A Wellington crew board their aircraft at dusk 'somewhere in England', July 1940. Night raids were becoming the norm for attacks on Germany by this date.

Vickers Wellington

Type:	Medium bomber
Engines:	Mk I 2 x 1,050 hp
	Bristol Pegasus XVIII
	Mk II 2 x 1,145 hp
	Rolls-Royce Merlin X
	Mk III 2 x 1,500 hp Bristol
	Hercules XI
Wingspan:	86 ft 2 in
Length:	64 ft 7 in
Height:	17 ft 5 in
Weight:	Empty 18,556 lb
	Loaded 29,500 lb
Armament:	6 (later 8) x 0.303 in machine guns in nose turret, tail turret
	and side windows
Bombload:	4,500 lb of bombs, or one mine or one torpedo
Max speed:	255 mph
Ceiling:	19,000 ft
Range:	2,200 miles
Production:	11,462

The Wellington was designed by the aircraft genius Barnes Wallis, later responsible for the bouncing bomb and other innovations. The most noticeable feature of the bomber was its astonishingly robust design, which allowed Wellingtons to fly safely home even when missing sections of wing or tail and with gaping holes in the fuselage. The strength was due to the geodetic framing devised by Barnes Wallis, though this flexible structure gave inexperienced crews frights as the wings wobbled alarmingly in flight. The Wellington entered service with the RAF in October 1938 and by December 1941 it comprised half the strength of Bomber Command, equipping 21 squadrons. As the new heavier bombers entered service in the bombing campaign against Germany, Wellingtons were moved to the Mediterranean and Far East theatres where they continued in service right to the end of the war.

Chapter 3

Massacre over Germany

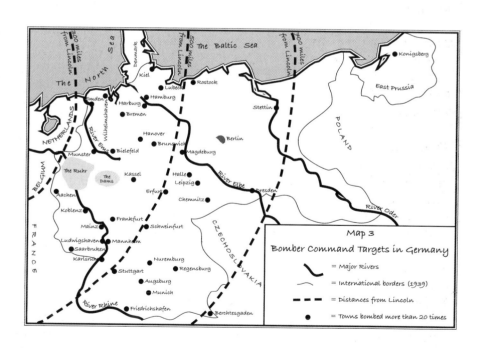

Map 3

Bomber Command Targets in Germany

$\displaystyle\sim$ = Major Rivers

$\longrightarrow$ = International borders (1939)

$---$ = Distances from Lincoln

● = Towns bombed more than 20 times

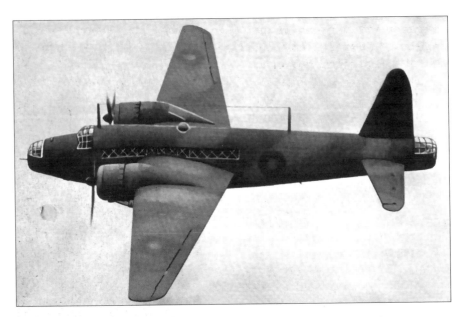

This postcard depicting a Wellington bomber was issued for sale to the patriotic public in 1941. Note that the front and rear turrets have been altered by airbrushing to innocuous domed windows for censorship purposes.

In June 1941 a train of events began that was to have a profound effect on the men of Bomber Command in Lincolnshire. A report landed on the desk of Lord Cherwell, Personal Scientific Adviser to Prime Minister Winston Churchill. The document related to cameras carried by the stripped down Spitfires of the Photo Reconnaissance Unit (PRU). But Lord Cherwell noticed something other than the technical merits of the various cameras. The photos taken showed much less damage to targets than had been reported by bomber crews. Cherwell called in Mr D. Butt of the Cabinet Secretariat. Two months later came the Butt Report, an in depth analysis of the effects of Bomber Command raids on Germany.

The Butt Report made disturbing reading. Butt discovered that only one third of bombers got within five miles of their target. Of these only a few actually hit the object of their raid. It was also found that the first bombs to hit a factory would destroy the walls and roofs, but that the heavy equipment within would usually be scarcely damaged. Only a second strike on the same spot could be relied upon to destroy the crucial manufacturing machines. For months the crews flying from Lincolnshire had known that navigation and bomb-aiming were both problems. Now the high command knew the full extent of those problems.

There were two immediate reactions. The first was to give an added boost to the development programme of new navigational aids. The need for equipment that would enable even relatively inexperienced men to navigate accurately hundreds of miles from home was clear. Fortunately technical aids were in the process of being produced. But it would be months before they could enter combat.

The second reaction was a decisive change in bombing tactics. Until the Butt Report, crews had been given very specific targets. They were asked to attack particular bridges, rail junctions or factories. Most bombs missed these targets and, in rural areas, fell on empty fields to do little damage except frighten a few cows. Portal and Peirse, head of

Air Marshal Sir Richard Peirse sits at his desk in Bomber Command Headquarters, High Wycombe.

operations at the Air Ministry, now adopted a new tactic that came to be known as 'area bombing'.

The basic premise was to choose an area in which there were several factories, rail junctions or other targets fairly close together. Crews would then be asked to hit the general area in the sure knowledge that there was a better chance of hitting something crucial than if the men were sent against single, isolated targets.

Soon a new fact came into the equation. Most suitable areas were located in towns and cities. These targets were, of course, surrounded by houses and other buildings. It was soon realised that by destroying houses, war production could be disrupted just as effectively as by hitting factories. With nowhere to live the workers could not go to their jobs. And the rubble created effectively blocked roads and rail links, further disrupting the war industries of Germany. The fact that area bombing would inevitably cause civilian casualties worried nobody. The only areas marked out for

E.V. Lawson, a pilot with 103 Squadron, poses proudly in the cockpit of his Wellington. Each of the bomb symbols painted on the fuselage indicates a mission successfully completed by the aircraft.
(David W. Fell and RAF Elsham Wolds Association)

such bombing were those engaged in war industries, and the only civilians in them were those engaged on war work. Such people were helping the German war machine just as much as were soldiers.

In this way, Bomber Command changed its tactics. The aircraft were now sent out against towns or cities rather than individual bridges or factories. The impact of Bomber Command's efforts increased substantially.

It was while returning from one of the earliest area bombing raids, on Duisburg late in August 1941, that the Hampden piloted by Sergeant Lyon of 106 Squadron was hit by flak over Holland. The aircraft did not seem to be badly damaged, so Lyon pressed on toward home. Suddenly both engines cut out. Despite Lyon's frantic efforts neither engine would restart and the Hampden began gliding down towards the dark waters of the North Sea.

Every bomber crew learned ditching procedure as part of its training, and given the long distances over sea flown during missions, they kept in constant practice. Assuming an aircraft was not too badly damaged, there would be two shocks as it hit the water. The first was a mild blow as the tail touched down, followed by a more violent blow as the front hit. There would then be up to five minutes, often less, before the aircraft sank. In that time each member of the crew had a specific job to do: to find the

The aircrew of 103 Squadron pose in front of a Wellington bomber in the summer of 1941. (David W. Fell and RAF Elsham Wolds Association)

food stores, to grab a map, to launch and inflate the dinghy, to get out of the aircraft, to help any wounded men to escape and finally to get into the dinghy and push off.

Raids could be very costly during the summer of 1941. On a single attack on 24 July 103 Squadron lost Sergeant Critchley (top left), Sergeant Bucknole (above) and Sergeant MacDonald (bottom, right of picture). None of the survivors of the raid saw these men crash so they were reported simply as 'Missing in Action'. Only when the months passed and the Germans failed to report them as prisoners did it become clear that they had been killed. (David W. Fell and RAF Elsham Wolds Association)

Fortunately Lyon's Hampden was intact and nobody was wounded. The four men got away in the dinghy. Knowing only that they were north of Holland, Lyon gave orders for the men to start paddling south. But soon cloud covered the stars, making it impossible to navigate, then heavy rain began to fall. All the next day and following night the rain fell, accompanied by dense cloud. The third day dawned bright and clear, but this only added sunburn and heat to the problems of the men. Lyon managed to rig a rudimentary sail from the crew's flying jackets as a north wind sprang up. The fourth day was hotter than the third, causing serious thirst problems.

On the fifth morning the wind got up and the waves increased dramatically in size. Suddenly a particularly large wave hit the dinghy, turning it over and pitching all four men into the sea. With amazement they realised the water was only four feet deep. As the tide fell, they found themselves on dry land. They were on a sand bank off the Dutch coast. A few hours later they were rescued by a small Dutch fishing boat, which took them ashore. By this point the men were in poor condition, so they decided to surrender to the Germans as the only way to get medical treatment. All four survived the war.

On the night of 7 November, the crews of Lincolnshire took part in what turned out to be one of the most critical raids of the war up to that date. The horrors of the night would long leave a scar on the collective memory of Bomber Command.

For over a year, Berlin, the capital of the Third Reich, had been on the list of approved targets for Bomber Command. The city was, however, both well defended and a long flight from Britain. As a result the raids had tended to be small scale and infrequent. Portal wrote: 'It is worth sacrificing ten tons of bombs from another target to get four million people out of bed and into the shelters.'

For the night of 7 November, Peirse decided to make a much larger effort. He and his staff were still reeling from the effects of the Butt Report, and wanted to prove that Bomber Command could achieve something worthwhile for the war effort. Indeed, Peirse decided to make a major effort – the largest of the war until then. No fewer than 392 bombers were scheduled to take off for Germany, of which 169 were heading for Berlin.

In Lincolnshire, 5 Group's Hampdens were given Berlin as a target even though this city was at the extreme range of their flying abilities. As the day wore on, the new 5 Group commander, Jack Slessor, became increasingly worried. His meteorological officer told him that strong westerly winds

Air Marshal Sir Richard Peirse (in cap) studies a mission map at Bomber Command Headquarters. To his right stands Sir Robert Saundby, who would later serve as deputy to Arthur Harris.

would set in overnight. Slessor worried that this would mean his crews flying home against a strong headwind with little fuel in their tanks.

By late afternoon, he had heard nothing from Peirse at Bomber Command HQ. Slessor therefore rang Peirse's office to explain his concerns. He asked if his bombers could be sent to the secondary target of Cologne instead. After some discussion, Peirse reluctantly agreed.

Slessor was not the only person worried. A station commander in 1 Group was also anxious. Although his men's Wellington bombers were better able to reach Berlin and return, doing so would take careful navigation in the face of the expected bad weather. On his own initiative, and risking disciplinary action, he stood down the less experienced crews and sent off only those he felt were able to do the job.

In the event the weather over Germany was even worse that Slessor had feared. As well as westerly winds, there were dense clouds of ice at bombing altitude. Many aircraft suffered severe icing problems on their wings, reducing speed and height while the engines were burning up more fuel. Of the bombers sent to Berlin an appalling 12.3% failed to return. Of those sent to Mannheim, 13% were lost. Worst of all was the fate of the force sent to drop mines in the Baltic: 21% of the aircraft failed to return. Only Slessor's men came back without loss. His prompt action had saved dozens of lives.

When Prime Minister Winston Churchill heard the news, his reaction was swift and decisive. He sent for Peirse and gave him new and clear orders. Bomber Command was to attack only targets that were easy to find, weakly defended or, preferably, both. Instead of undertaking costly raids that produced little result, Bomber Command was to concentrate on training new crews, acquiring new equipment and improving navigation.

German civilians clear rubble from a Berlin street after the raid of 7 November. Damage inflicted was light, but Bomber Command took heavy losses.

Ground crew at work on a Stirling. This was the first of the four-engined bombers to enter service, but proved to be disappointing and was swiftly relegated to training duties.

Thus, Churchill believed, spring 1942 would see a rejuvenated and greatly strengthened Bomber Command ready to launch an effective assault on the enemy.

One of the new aircraft then entering service was the Avro Manchester. This two-engined bomber was designed to take over from the Hampden and was reckoned to be at least the equal of the reliable Wellington. It proved to be quite otherwise, and some Lincolnshire crews soon regretted handing in their Hampdens. Rather more promising, at least at first, was the Short Stirling. Both aircraft went into service with 5 Group as the Hampdens were phased out. The men of 1 Group continued to fly their Wellingtons. It was with these aircraft that the men of Bomber Command, Lincolnshire, flew their missions for months to come.

One of the first missions flown with the new aircraft took place late in December when 49 Squadron, recently equipped with Manchesters, was sent on a daylight raid against a German fighter base near the Dutch coast. The raid was timed to take place at sunset with the bombers flying in low from the west. By flying low over the North Sea it was hoped they would evade enemy radar while the approach from the setting sun would stop them being seen by the Luftwaffe men on the ground.

Initially the plan worked perfectly and the Manchesters roared in over the Luftwaffe base at a height of 100 feet without being seen. The aircraft flown by Pilot Officer Ronald Robinson had the misfortune to have its bomb-aimer's cockpit shattered by a bird as it began its bombing run. Nevertheless, the crew dropped its bombs on a hangar with deadly accuracy while the gunners hosed bullets at the buildings and parked Messerschmitt 109 fighters beneath them.

As Robinson pulled up and away to give his rear gunner a clear aim, a shell exploded inside the bomb-aimer's cockpit. The bomb-aimer was killed and a fire started, spreading rapidly back along the fuselage. Although he was now, quite literally, sitting on top of a fire, Robinson calmly piloted his aircraft towards home while his gunners struggled to get the flames under control. Crossing the Kent coast with smoke pouring from his aircraft, Robinson decided to land at the first airbase he saw. As he came in to land Robinson realised the undercarriage would not work, so he performed a belly landing that tore the floor from his aircraft. Other than the unfortunate bomb-aimer, the entire crew escaped without a scratch.

Meanwhile, Portal had found the time to launch his own investigation into the disastrous raids on 7 November. He had at first accepted Peirse's explanation that the losses resulted from unexpectedly bad weather. But in December he spoke to Slessor and found out about 5 Group's change of plan based on the local weather report. Portal looked at the weather reports that had been given to Peirse on the afternoon of the raid and found that they, too, forecast strong westerly winds and bad weather. Not only had Peirse sent his force off in the face of such adverse weather, but he had tried to cover up the facts afterwards.

On 4 January Portal went to see Churchill. Again, Churchill acted swiftly and decisively. Peirse was moved on 8 January to take command of the air force in India. Bomber Command needed a new commander, but until a permanent replacement could be found Air Vice Marshal Jack Baldwin of 3 Group took over temporarily. It was during Baldwin's time that the bomber crews of Lincolnshire were called on to undertake an emergency mission that proved to be one of the most dramatic of the war.

The prelude to the action took place in December 1941, when Peirse still led Bomber Command. A force of Wellingtons was sent to Brest once again to attack the powerful German warships that lurked there and posed a potent threat to Atlantic convoys. One aircraft of 144 Squadron was piloted by Pilot Officer George Glenn and navigated by Pilot Officer Duncan Miller. Unusually for this date the raid was to be carried out in daylight to ensure accurate bombing, so important were these targets deemed to be.

The accuracy of Miller's navigation was such that when Glenn dived down through the low cloud he found himself right above Brest. Turning quickly to line up on the warships, Glenn ran his starboard wing into a balloon cable. The cable sliced the end off the wing and slewed the bomber round to the extent that it was flying almost sideways. Wrestling with the control column, Glenn got his Wellington back on an even keel just as an anti-aircraft shell exploded immediately above the port tail plane. Again the aircraft veered wildly out of control. Again the pilot managed to get the bomber back on course. The bombs were dropped, though nobody on board saw how they fell.

Climbing rapidly away from Brest, Glenn found he could just about keep the aircraft on course and called on Miller to plot a course for the nearest point in England. The crew prepared to bail out if, as seemed likely, the aircraft should become too dangerous to fly. With the controls dragging all the time and the tail threatening to fall off, the plane flew sluggishly over Brittany and the Channel. It was with relief that the crew saw Cornwall appear beneath them. Miller navigated them down to a small aerodrome, where Glenn managed to put the aircraft down in one piece. The Wellington was so badly damaged that it was scrapped.

Meanwhile, the normal run of wartime missions continued. On 10 January 1942 103 Squadron took part in a relatively routine sortie to bomb the Ruhr. If the mission was unexceptional, its aftermath was to become the stuff of legend. Squadron Leader Ian Cross, leader of B Flight, was shot down as he approached the target. Baling out, Cross and his crew were taken prisoner by the Germans. After an active career in 'goon baiting', the teasing of German camp guards, Cross found himself moved to Stalag Luft III. This base was run by the Luftwaffe and was reserved for troublesome prisoners, such as Cross.

In Stalag Luft III, Cross met several veterans of Lincolnshire, among them Brian H. Evans of 49 Squadron, James L.R. Long of 9 Squadron, George E. McGill of 103 Squadron, Rupert J. Stevens of 12 Squadron, Richard S.A. Churchill of 144 Squadron, Leslie C. Brodrick of 106 Squadron and Bertram A. James MC again of 9 Squadron. The key figure in what was to follow, however, was a fighter pilot: Squadron Leader Roger Bushell. It was Bushell's idea to halt the various escape attempts and concentrate all efforts on a single, mass escape. He hoped to get no fewer than 200 men out in a single night. The plan came to be known as The Great Escape.

Almost every one of the 600 prisoners in the camp had a role to play, whether as a tailor making civilian clothes, a forger producing fake papers or as diggers working on the tunnels. Cross was put in charge of the so-called 'penguins', men who secretly disposed of the soil dug out of the tunnels in a way so that the guards did not spot it. The name came from the odd waddling gait the men adopted when walking with sacks of soil stuffed down their trouser legs.

Of the three tunnels that were begun, one collapsed and a second was discovered by the Germans. The third tunnel, named 'Harry', was completed on 14 March 1944. The escape was scheduled for ten days later and the 200 escapers were selected, equipped with clothes and papers, then given final instructions. In the event the tunnel was found to end short of a protective screen of trees and only 76 men got out before the Germans discovered the tunnel exit.

Just three men got back to Britain safely, all the rest being recaptured over the following weeks. Fifteen men were returned to the camp, two were sent to Colditz and another was held in prison in Berlin.

On 6 April the Camp Commandant, Oberst Braune, called the senior

Navigator Flight Lieutenant Yarker (left) always steered his Wellington, piloted by Reggie Fulbrook (right) over Oxfordshire on their outbound flights so that he could wave to his fiancée. (David W. Fell and RAF Elsham Wolds Association)

British officer in the camp, Group Captain Massey, to his office. Relations between prisoners and guards had been difficult since the escape, but it was at once obvious to Massey that something was seriously wrong. Braune was quite obviously upset and it was with a clear reluctance that he announced that he was ordered to inform the British officer that 50 of the escaped officers had been recaptured and then shot whilst trying to escape.

Massey couldn't believe it. 'How many were wounded?' he asked.

'None,' replied Braune, 'and I am not permitted to give you any further information, except that their bodies and effects will be returned to you.'

It later became clear that the men had been murdered by the Gestapo on the personal orders of SS chief Heinrich Himmler, acting with Hitler's authority. All the ringleaders, including Cross, had been singled out for death. The surviving prisoners at Stalag Luft III were allowed by Braune to erect a memorial in the camp, and this was moved to a nearby cemetery when the camp was demolished in 1946. After the war an investigation was held and the 21 Gestapo men who had carried out the killings were executed.

A few nights after Cross had taken off on his fateful mission, 103 Squadron at Elsham Wolds gained a new crew led by Flight Lieutenant Yarker and Reggie Fulbrook. These two men had been crack officers in the pre-war RAF and had spent the war so far training crews, in particular teaching Czechs and Poles how to fly RAF machines. Now they gained a posting to an operational squadron for the first time.

At this point in the war, the routes taken by bombers were still a matter for the crews themselves, so Yarker steered Fulbrook south over Henley. The Wellington usually passed over the town as dusk drew in, allowing Yarker to wave to his fiancée who stood in her garden each evening to see if he flew over.

One raid carried out by the crew was on the Ford factory at Poissy, near Paris, where the Germans were using French labour to build panzers. The

Ian Cross (left), shot down over the Ruhr on 10 January 1942, would later play a leading role in the daring plan to break out of a prisoner of war camp that was to become immortalised in the movie The Great Escape. *Another escaper was George E. McGill (right), another hero of Bomber Command who had been flying from Lincolnshire when he was shot down.*
(David W. Fell and RAF Elsham Wolds Association)

briefing officer told the assembled bomb-aimers of 103 Squadron, 'You can't miss it, it's the tallest building there.'

As Fulbrook approached the area he saw the tall factory building, announced 'Turning on target' and sent Yarker down to his bomb-aiming position. What had not been mentioned in the briefing was that there were three flak guns on the factory roof. Tracer from the three guns converged on the Wellington, which felt as if a giant's hand had suddenly reached out and stopped it in midair. Yarker released the bombs, then turned around to see the fuselage behind him a mass of flames.

A shell had fractured the hydraulic system and a spray of burning oil was playing along the fabric covering of the Wellington's fuselage. Yarker emptied a fire extinguisher on the blaze, then resorted to beating at the fire with his flying gloves. The fire was eventually put out, but the loss of the hydraulic fluid meant that the wheels and flaps were hanging down, making the aircraft almost unmanageable. By the time the plane got back to Lincolnshire, it was barely able to hold height and Fulbrook had to veer wildly to avoid a church steeple as he approached base.

The following night the crew went out for a drink in a local pub, to be told that the previous evening a low flying bomber had knocked off the pub's chimney pot. Yarker and Fulbrook decided to keep quiet.

Both men were awarded DFCs for their actions. Fulbrook was later killed on a training flight, but Yarker survived the war and entered civil aviation. He retired in 1961.

It was on 11 February that the men of Lincolnshire were called upon to undertake an emergency mission to put right mistakes made elsewhere. It was one of the county's finest hours.

Just before midnight on 11 February the powerful German battlecruisers *Scharnhorst* and *Gneisenau* left the French port of Brest together with the heavy cruiser *Prinz Eugen*. The Germans had decided that the big ships were too exposed at Brest after the raid in which Miller and Glenn had taken part. The vessels were to be moved back to Germany ready to steam either to the Baltic to face the Russian fleet or to attack the Arctic convoys off Norway. The Germans decided to risk making a high-speed voyage along the English Channel rather than taking the long route around Iceland and down the Norwegian coast. They gave the operation the codename 'Cerberus', but it is better known as the Channel Dash.

Bad weather covered Brest, so the reconnaissance flights flown by the RAF at dawn on 12 February failed to show that the ships had gone.

Furthermore the lookouts of the Royal Navy submarine patrolling off Brest saw nothing. It was not until 11.25 next morning that an RAF Spitfire pilot returning from a routine patrol reported German ships in the Channel. This caused the Navy to send out a small fleet of destroyers from Harwich. These ships were promptly attacked by RAF bombers from southern England, which mistook them for the German ships. The destroyers then headed for the wrong position, their navigation officer having made a mistake on his charts.

By this time there was growing panic that the German ships would get back to Germany undamaged. Finally the squadrons of 5 Group were called upon to take a hand.

A reconnaissance photo showing the German battlecruiser Gneisenau *at sea. She is indicated at 1, while escorting destroyers appear at 2.*

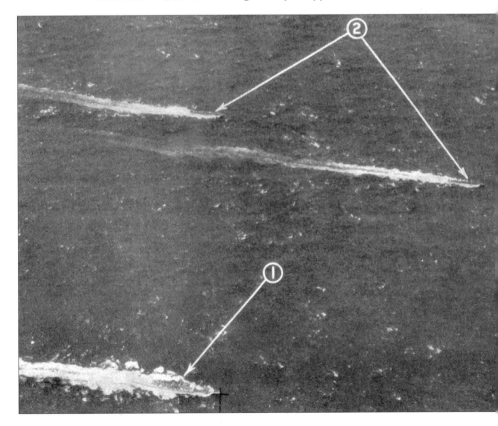

First into the air was 83 Squadron taking off from Scampton in the much disliked Manchester bombers. Flying at less than 1,000 feet to stay beneath the blanket of dense cloud, the Manchesters located the German warships and went straight into the attack. At once the protective umbrella of German Messerschmitt 109 fighters zeroed in on the bombers. Three of the fighters made for the aircraft flown by Pilot Officer Robert McFarlane. Despite his low altitude, McFarlane threw his aircraft around the sky as if performing aerobatics. At one point his upper gunner managed to get an accurate burst of fire in on one of the fighters, which, with its companions, broke off the attack.

McFarlane then pushed on with his attack, although he was now behind the main formation. As he neared the zig-zagging ships he came under intense anti-aircraft fire. The plane's twin rudders were riddled with shot to the extent that they became virtually useless while a shell exploded alongside and tore a huge hole in the fabric of the fuselage.

Not until he was over the ships did McFarlane realise that his aircraft's hydraulic system had been destroyed, making it impossible to open the bomb doors. Unable to bomb his target, McFarlane turned for home. A shell burst just below the rear of the aircraft, tearing another great hole in the fuselage.

Realising that he would be lucky to get back to Lincolnshire, McFarlane headed for the nearest airbase and put his crippled Manchester down to a bumpy landing. An inspection next day showed that shrapnel from the final shell burst had sliced through the elevator cables, leaving this vital control wire connected by just two thin strands of wire. McFarlane was promptly given a bar to the DFC that he had won only three weeks earlier on a raid over Germany.

A mere 20 minutes after the Manchesters of 144 Squadron had completed their attack, the Wellingtons of 12 Squadron flying from Binbrook came in to launch their own onslaught. Again, the approach was made below the cloud cover as soon as the squadron sighted the ships. The first aircraft in was flown by Pilot Officer Norman Richardson, who dived down to just 400 feet above the sea to make certain of a good view for his bomb-aimer.

As the Wellington approached the *Gneisenau* a shell burst in front of the cockpit. The flash of the explosion temporarily blinded Richardson, while a red hot fragment of shell casing tore into his forearm. Nevertheless, Richardson held his aircraft steady while the bombs were dropped, exploding just yards from the cruiser's bow and, as it later transpired, buckling some plates to such an extent that seawater gushed in.

The bomb-aimer clambered into the shattered cockpit to administer first aid in the shape of a bandage around Richardson's arm. Undeterred, Richardson flew home to Binbrook. He was awarded the second DFC to be won that day by men of Lincolnshire.

Next, 103 Squadron was sent out on a 'gardening' mission to lay mines in the North Sea ahead of the German ships. Flying low across the North Sea in appalling weather, the aircraft laid a pattern of mines with great precision. The *Gneisenau* hit a mine and, although she limped into Kiel for repairs, never put to sea again. The *Scharnhorst* struck two mines, but neither inflicted serious damage and in January 1943 she steamed north to Norway to attack the Arctic convoys as planned.

One of the men engaged on this 'gardening' mission was Tom Sadler, flying as a front gunner with 103 Squadron out of Elsham

Tom Sadler, famed for his cool, unflappable temperament when in combat first took to the war-torn skies over Germany at the unusually advanced age of 31. (David W. Fell and RAF Elsham Wolds Association)

Wolds. Sadler had qualified as an Air Gunner in June 1941 at the unusually advanced age of 31. Sadler flew in Wellingtons throughout his career and was much in demand since his aim was as faultless as his coolness in action. Sadler flew 32 operations with 103 Squadron with 8 different crews before transferring to training duties. Even then he took part in occasional operational flights before moving to North Africa to take part in another 32 operations. He survived the war.

In February 1942 a change came over Bomber Command that was to have an immediate and dramatic impact on the men flying from Lincolnshire. The new commander of Bomber Command took office. The man who stepped into the shoes vacated by Peirse was none other than the former commander of 5 Group. Brought back from America, Arthur Harris was given the task of turning Bomber Command around and making it a truly war winning weapon.

He didn't waste much time.

Avro Manchester

Type:	Heavy bomber
Engines:	2 x 1,760 hp
	Rolls-Royce Vulture
Wingspan:	90 ft 1 in
Length:	68 ft 10 in
Height:	19 ft 6 in
Weight:	Empty 29,440 lb
	Loaded 50,000 lb
Armament:	8 x 0.303 machine guns
	in nose, dorsal and tail turrets
Bombload:	10,350 lb of bombs
Max speed:	265 mph
Ceiling:	19,200 ft
Range:	1,630 miles
Production:	201

The Manchester was a classic example of an aircraft that looked magnificent on the design board, but proved to be a failure in action. With a heavy bomb load the aircraft should have been a useful weapon of war while the gun turret on the top of the aircraft should have provided additional defence, as should the rear turret, which carried four machine guns in place of the usual two. However, the sturdy, well-designed fuselage and wings were let down by the engines. These proved to be dangerously unreliable and prone to bursting into flames at high revs. Directional instability forced Avro to add a third central tail fin to later production aircraft, and to make the tail planes larger. Only a few months after entering combat, the Manchester was withdrawn from service.

Short Stirling

Type:	Heavy bomber
Engines:	4 x 1,600 hp Bristol Hercules XI
Wingspan:	99 ft 1 in
Length:	87 ft 3 in
Height:	22 ft 9 in
Weight:	Empty 44,000 lb
	Loaded 70,000 lb
Armament:	8 x 0.303 in machine guns in nose, dorsal and tail turrets
Bombload:	14,000 lb of bombs
Max speed:	270 mph
Ceiling:	17,000 ft
Range:	2,010 miles
Production:	2,371

The Stirling got off to a bad start in May 1939 when the first prototype crashed on its maiden flight. Redesign followed, producing the final shape of this the first four-engined bomber to enter service with the RAF. It was introduced amid high hopes that it would prove to be a decisive aircraft for Bomber Command. It could carry a heavier bomb load than any other aircraft in service and had a useful range, enabling it to reach many targets. Later in the war the low ceiling began to cause problems, as did the layout of the bomb bay, which meant the Stirling could carry only smaller bombs. In 1943 the aircraft began to be replaced as a bomber. The existing Stirlings were converted to be glider tugs or long-distance transport aircraft.

Chapter 4

The Augsburg Raid

When Air Marshal Arthur Harris took up his postion as head of Bomber Command on 22 February 1942 he found an urgent order lying on his desk in High Wycombe. Dated one week earlier, the directive came from Air Marshal Portal, head of the Air Staff in London. At first sight it appeared self-contradictory.

The order began by repeating the already established policy of 'area bombing', naming four cities – Essen, Duisburg, Dusseldorf and Cologne – as the prime targets with fourteen others as secondary targets. The bombing of these cites was, Harris was told, his 'primary objective'. However the instructions went on to accord 'top priority' to eight specific targets, made up of four power stations, three oil plants and one rubber factory.

The entrance to the underground planning room at Bomber Command HQ. As shown here, a sentry was on duty 24 hours a day throughout the war.

The underground planning room at Bomber Command HQ in High Wycombe. It was here that major raids, such as that at Augsburg, were planned and supervised.

The Lancaster 'Just Jane' that is preserved at East Kirby airfield as the star exhibit of the Lincolnshire Aviation Centre. (http://www.oldairfields.fotopic.net/)

The key to Portal's thinking in formulating this order was the development of a new, top secret navigational aid codenamed 'Gee'. In 1940 the task of solving the chronic problems of navigating bombers at night over enemy territory had been given to Robert Dippy of the Telecommunications Research Establishment (TRE). After a year's work, Dippy produced the answer. He developed a 'Gee Box' that could be carried in a bomber and operated by a navigator after only minimal training.

The box received radio pulses sent out at regular intervals by three powerful transmitters in England, each 100 miles from the other. The pulses were sent out at precisely the same instant by the transmitters, but would arrive fractions of a second apart at the receiving box. A simple triangulation carried out on the signals would give the navigator his position. Dippy estimated the equipment accurate to just 100 yards at a range of 350 miles. He also estimated that it would take the Germans about six months to produce effective countermeasures from the time they first captured an intact 'Gee Box' from a downed bomber. Crews were given strict instructions to destroy the 'Gee Box' if they were forced to land in enemy territory, but even so it would be only a matter of time before the Germans got hold of one.

As well as Gee, Bomber Command was getting new models of aircraft. The most impressive of these was the Lancaster. This four-engined bomber could carry a heavy bombload, was armed with eight machine guns and would soon prove to be one of the most reliable aircraft in the world. It was the RAF's finest bomber.

At the time, however, nobody was entirely certain how this superlative machine would perform in combat. After including a small number of Lancasters on routine night raids on Essen (25 March) and Lübeck (28 March), Air Marshal Harris decided to try a new tactic.

Many senior staff at the Air Ministry still held to the belief of Sir Hugh Trenchard, Chief of the Air Staff in the 1920s, that properly organised bomber formations could fight their way through enemy fighters in daylight. This would enable the bombers to identify and hit specific targets accurately, thus ending the dropping of large numbers of bombs which fell harmlessly in open countryside or on houses rather than war industry factories. These men, of which Archibald Sinclair, Air Minister, was one, argued that the appalling casualties suffered during daylight raids earlier in the war had been due to inexperienced crews and inadequate aircraft.

The new Lancaster could fly further and faster than the earlier twin-engined aircraft, and had twice as many machine guns. With skilled crews, it was suggested, the new aircraft would be able to penetrate enemy air space, deliver a precision attack and get back without undue loss. It was also pointed out that with the new 'Gee' navigation equipment there was less chance of the aircraft getting lost and wasting time cruising around looking for the target.

Harris came under great pressure to test these theories in combat. He chose as the target for a one-off daylight raid the MAN factory at Augsburg in Bavaria. These works were turning out diesel engines for the U-boats that were at that time decimating Atlantic convoys. It had long a priority target for Bomber Command, but the site was difficult to locate at night and the factory so small that the chances of a direct hit in the dark were effectively nil. A daylight raid seemed the only way to secure a good chance of causing serious damage.

So far as can be made out from the contemporary paperwork, Harris was not convinced of the theory. He arranged for the raid to hit its target at dusk, so that the bombers would have the cover of night for their return journey. To aid them on the outward journey, Harris ordered more than a hundred medium bombers to strike at targets in France and the Low Countries to distract the German defences and keep their fighters busy. Finally, he ordered the crews undertaking the mission to fly as low as possible to evade German radar.

To go on this raid, Harris selected Squadron Leader John Dering Nettleton of 44 Squadron, based at Waddington, with Squadron Leader Jack Sherwood of 97 Squadron at Woodhall Spa acting as his second in command. Both were highly experienced commanders and both squadrons had been flying Lancasters in training for several weeks. Harris clearly felt that if anyone could make the 1,250 mile round trip with any chance of

An unidentified Group HQ in 1942. It was from here that authorisation to proceed with raids was given.

A squadron operations room. It was here that the technical details of a raid, including routes and flight times were worked out.

success, it was these Lincolnshire-based bomber crews.

Nettleton was to lead the raid. He had been born on 28 June 1917 in Nongoma, South Africa, as the son and grandson of officers in the Royal Navy. He trained as a sea officer on leaving school, but his first love was always flying rather than sailing. In 1938 he decided to join the RAF, travelling to Britain to do so in October. He was accepted as an officer and began pilot training, from which he graduated on 22 July 1939. After a short spell of operational flying with 98 Squadron, he served as a pilot instructor for almost two years, returning to active flying at 44 Squadron in July 1941.

By the time Nettleton was selected to lead the Augsburg Raid he had already been mentioned in despatches and completed a tour of duty. On 12 April 1942 Nettleton was told to select six crews for intensive practice in daylight formation flying at low level, but was not told of the reason for this. Nor was he told why six aircraft of 97 Squadron were joining the flights. On each of the following four days the twelve Lancasters took off for hour after hour of exhausting low-level practice, and each night the ground crews were kept hard at work correcting the slightest fault in the aircraft.

On the morning of 17 April, Nettleton was told that the mission would be undertaken that afternoon, and was finally informed of the target. He at once cancelled that day's training flight and advised his men to get as much rest as they could. Nettleton himself went to see the ground crews and ensured that every aircraft was in as near perfect condition as possible.

At lunchtime the aircraft began to be loaded with four 1,000 lb bombs each while the crews went for their briefing.

At 3.12 pm Nettleton lifted off and began circling Waddington at low level while his other aircraft took off and grouped up in formation. Nettleton chose to adopt a double V formation. In front was himself, flanked by two other Lancasters flying slightly behind him. These were piloted by Warrant Officer G.T. Rhodes and Flying Officer J. Garwell DFC. A short distance behind came a second V of three aircraft piloted by Flight Lieutenant N. Sandford, Warrant Officer J.E. Beckett and Warrant Officer H.V. Crum. A seventh aircraft followed behind to take the place of any plane that developed mechanical failure, but it turned back over the Channel when it was clear all was well.

As the Lancasters thundered south over Lincolnshire they were joined by Sherwood's six aircraft from Woodhall Spa. Keeping strict radio silence, the formation crossed the Channel at wave-top height, then roared over the French coast and pushed on inland. All seemed to be going as hoped. There was no sign of any German aircraft nor of any flak. Clearly the diversionary raids organised by Harris were doing their job. At this point, Nettleton's six aircraft from 44 Squadron began to pull ahead of the 97 Squadron aircraft to follow a slightly more southern route. The move was to prove fatal.

As Nettleton's formation raced across France they had the misfortune to pass close to Beaumont-le-Roger, then the base for the Luftwaffe's Fighter Squadron No 2, equipped with Messerschmitt Bf109 aircraft. The squadron was led by the hugely experienced Hauptmann Oesau, who had already clocked up 100 'kills' during the Battle of Britain and over Russia. He habitually flew an aircraft painted jet black throughout and ensured that all his squadron's aircraft had black on them somewhere, despite official regulations demanding camouflage paint schemes.

Oesau, returning from fighting off one of Harris's diversionary raids, was leading his men in to land when he saw the six Lancasters passing at low level. He ordered his tired men to climb back into the air and follow him in pursuit. Low on fuel and ammunition, the Germans could keep up the chase for only 10 minutes. It was enough.

Beckett's Lancaster was the first to be hit. It was raked from end to end by cannonfire from two German fighter planes, and dived straight into the ground, exploding instantly. Sandford's aircraft was attacked next, the fuel tanks exploding with a blinding flash in mid air. Crum was third in line, his engines being set on fire in seconds. Crum hurriedly dumped his bombs then, wrestling gallantly with his crippled aircraft, managed to pancake down in an open field. He and his crew, several of whom were injured, scrambled clear to spend the rest of the war as prisoners.

The fourth Lancaster to be hit was attacked by Oesau himself. Rhodes' aircraft was struck by cannonfire and the nose pulled up with savage force. It then veered to the right and dived past Nettleton's aircraft to hit the ground vertically with all engines roaring at full throttle.

At this point the Germans pulled out of the attack due to lack of fuel, leaving the two surviving Lancasters to continue on towards Augsburg. Forming up wingtip to wingtip, Nettleton and Garwell came in at about 200 feet over the roofs of Augsburg. Both aircraft put their bombs straight into the factory complex, then climbed for height. Garwell proved to be unlucky; his Lancaster was hit by flak which knocked out two engines and started a fire in the port wing. Too low to bale out, Garwell crash-landed. Three of his crew died, but the rest survived.

As Nettleton was escaping, Sherwood led the six aircraft from 97 Squadron into the attack. Following the bomb bursts caused by 44 Squadron, Sherwood came in even lower. The Lancaster flown by Warrant Officer Mycock was hit and exploded in mid air over the town, while a second, piloted by Flying Officer E.A. Deverill, was set on fire. Deverill continued his run in formation to plant his bombs in the MAN complex. The Lancaster flown by Squadron Leader David Penman was hit repeatedly and two gunners badly injured, but he too continued into the attack.

As the surviving aircraft of 97 Squadron pulled away, Sherwood's Lancaster was hit three times in quick succession by flak. Totally out of control, the bomber nosed into the ground in the middle of a street and exploded into a vast orange fireball. Astonishingly, Sherwood was thrown clear by the impact and hurtled through the air to have his fall cushioned by the branches of a street-side tree. He was found, unconscious and badly wounded, by a German civilian about half an hour later.

The return journey was less horrific than the outbound trip, the darkness protecting the Lancasters from the attentions of the Luftwaffe. Unfortunately, Nettleton's navigational equipment had been knocked out so he had to fly home on dead reckoning. After some heart-stopping moments, Nettleton spotted an airfield and put his Lancaster down almost empty of fuel. It turned out he was at Squire's Gate in Lancashire.

Squadron Leader Penman, meanwhile, had formed up with Deverill's damaged aircraft as they left Augsburg. Deverill had only three engines working and, although he had managed to extinguish the fire, there was a 10 ft gash down the side of his aircraft. Ignoring the chance to fly home at speed, Penman chose to stay with Deverill to help drive off any German fighters that might arrive and also to report the position if Deverill had to ditch in the sea. The two aircraft limped home to Woodhall Spa some two hours after the other two survivors from 97 Squadron had landed.

The results of the raid were spectacular. Seventeen of the 1,000 lb bombs had hit the factory, causing widespread damage that took months to put right. It was later discovered that there were four other factories making U-boat engines, so the impact on U-boat production was not as great as Harris proclaimed immediately after the raid. Nonetheless, the raid did force the Germans to divert resources into the manufacture of anti-aircraft guns to ring even their most isolated factories.

On a personal level, Nettleton was awarded the Victoria Cross for his exploits. Although Harris recommended Sherwood for the same award, he was given the Distinguished Service Order, while Penman and Deverill were also both awarded the DSO.

The cost, however, had been too high. The casualty rate for the raid was a crippling 58% at a time when Harris considered 4% to be the maximum acceptable for a routine mission and 20% for a special target. Harris drew the obvious lesson that the new fast, heavily-armed bombers were still too vulnerable to use in daylight raids over Germany. He gave strict instructions that no such raids were take place again.

Of the medal winning heroes of the raid, Sherwood spent the rest of the war as a prisoner while Deverill was too badly wounded to fly operationally again and was transferred to training duties. Nettleton was promoted to Wing Commander and given command of 44 Squadron. On 12 July 1943 he was shot down over Turin and killed just a few weeks before his son was to be born.

Penman went on to have a lengthy active service. Having been flying in the RAF since 1938, he completed his second tour of operational duty in 1943 with a DFC to add to the DSO won at Augsburg. He then spent two years training bomber pilots before transferring to Burma to fly transport aircraft supplying the 14th Army in its advance to Rangoon. After the war he stayed in the East, flying many hazardous supply missions during the troublesome period leading up to independence for India, Pakistan and Burma. He had the distinction of being the last RAF pilot to fly out of India in January 1948. After that, Penman served with the RAF in Germany as the Cold War with the Soviet Union took hold and later took over flight training of teenagers in the Air Training Corps. He finally retired from the RAF in 1984 having completed 48 years of service and gaining an OBE for his devotion to duty. He died in November 2004.

One of the second pilots flying with the 44 Squadron aircraft was Patrick Dorehill. He too was awarded a DFC for the action. In March 1944 Dorehill was to win a second DFC, again when serving with 44 Squadron. He was flying to Berlin when attacked by a night-fighter. Although the bomber was repeatedly hit by cannonfire, losing the hydraulic system, Dorehill flew on to bomb Berlin and return to Lincolnshire. The aircraft was a write off.

Meanwhile, the bomber squadrons of Lincolnshire returned to the night-bombing offensive. And soon they would be taking part in the biggest raid of the entire war. It was time for the 'Thousand Bomber Raids'.

Avro Lancaster

Type:	Heavy bomber
Engines:	Model B1 4 x 1,280 hp
	Rolls-Royce Merlin Mk20
	Model B2 4 x 1,675 hp
	Bristol Hercules VI
Wingspan:	102 ft
Length:	68 ft 10 in
Height:	20 ft 4 in
Weight:	Empty 41,000 lb
	Loaded 68,000 lb
Armament:	8 x 0.303 in machine guns: 2 in nose turret,
	2 in dorsal turret, 4 in tail turret
Bombload:	14,000 lb
Max speed:	287 mph
Ceiling:	24,500 ft
Range:	2,678 miles
Production:	7,377

The Lancaster was the most successful British bomber of the Second World War. It was developed by Avro from the earlier Manchester, whose two engines proved to be seriously underpowered. The addition of two additional engines meant the aircraft required longer wings, but otherwise it remained effectively the same. The first prototype flew on 9 January 1941 and production began that October. The first aircraft was delivered to an operational squadron in March 1942, but engine shortages meant it was many months before it was available in large numbers. As well as the standard B1 and B2 models, the Lancaster was produced in a variety of special configurations, most notably the 23 aircraft built with larger bomb bays and no dorsal turret to undertake the Dambusters Raid. After the war large numbers of Lancasters were converted to Lincoln passenger aircraft or Lancastrian cargo carriers and sold off to a variety of airlines in many different countries. Today only one Lancaster remains in flying condition – that is with the RAF Battle of Britain flight – but a number of others are able to taxi and several are on static display in museums.

Chapter 5

The 'Heavies' come to Lincolnshire

A photograph taken by an aircraft of 103 Squadron on its run in to attack Dortmund in May 1943. (David W. Fell and RAF Elsham Wolds Association)

A postcard sold in 1942 that describes the Wellington bomber as a 'heavy' bomber. In fact by this date the RAF had redesignated all twin-engined bombers as 'mediums'.

After the Augsburg Raid, Arthur Harris decided to devote his squadrons to the 'area bombing' attacks that had already proved themselves to be reasonably effective and less costly than other tactics. His orders were to degrade the capacity of German industry to produce weapons and supplies that would keep the vast armed forces of the Wehrmacht in the field. That meant bombing industrial cities, and Harris took on the task with skill and dedication.

Several reforms begun under Peirse and Portal reached fruition during the early months of Harris's command. The most noticeable of these came in the form of the big four-engined bombers. These aircraft, the Stirling, Halifax and Lancaster, could carry heavier bombs in greater numbers over longer distances with more reliability than the two-engined aircraft they replaced.

Almost as significant were the improvements to navigation. Primarily this was 'Gee', which, as we have seen in Chapter 4, enabled a navigator to fix his aircraft's position with reasonable accuracy if less than 350 miles from England by means of triangulating radio beams. New navigation aids,

The remains of the north runway at Kelstern airfield. Existing runways had to be extended in 1942 to give the four-engined bombers enough room to take off. (http://www.oldairfields.fotopic.net/)

A 1942 taxi route leads to a hangar at Spilsby. The larger bombers required larger hangars, many of which survive to serve as farm buildings or industrial workshops. (http://www.oldairfields.fotopic.net/)

which would enter service as 'Oboe' and 'H2S', were under development, though they would not be used until the end of 1942.

Less obvious were changes in tactics and organisation. One plan that Harris opposed was to put only one pilot in each aircraft. This enabled twice as many aircraft to take off as when two pilots were in each aircraft. Harris insisted that another crew member had to be trained well enough to pilot the aircraft home in an emergency and that an automatic pilot, codenamed 'George', had to be fitted.

A change that did receive Harris's enthusiastic backing was 'streaming'. Previously each bomber had been free to choose its own route to the target and, except in a few cases, to deliver its attack at the time and height the pilot preferred. However, casualties caused by night-fighters and anti-aircraft guns had been rising steadily as the Germans became experienced in the difficult skills of accurate shooting in the dark.

Henceforth the bombers were to be organised in a stream. This meant that every bomber had to follow the same route to and from the target, flying at a similar height and time to all the others. It was hoped that the enemy fighters and gunners would no longer be able to pick off the bombers one by one as they made their attacks but, instead, would be swamped by a vast number of attackers arriving at once. There were initial fears that bombers would collide in the dark, but such casualties proved to be far less than the numbers saved from German attacks.

At first the bomber streams were haphazard and only loosely organised. Eventually that would change and develop, until by 1945 every single bomber had its allotted time and height over the target. Streaming proved to be among the most effective defensive tactics adopted by Bomber Command.

Harris also oversaw an extensive reconstruction programme in Lincolnshire. Airfields were massively rebuilt, mostly on a standard pattern. Runways and taxi routes were laid out in solid concrete and were surrounded by standardised lighting layouts. Thus even a pilot who had never been to a base before would be familiar with the layout and be unlikely to cause an accident through ignorance.

In May 1942 Harris decided that the new tactics, aircraft and men were ready to be called upon to face a stern test. On 18 May he went to see Portal with a breathtaking idea. He wanted to send 1,000 bombers to pound either Hamburg or Cologne, both crucial industrial centres that were easy to locate.

Elsham Wolds airfield seen from the air during the war. The three-runway layout was typical of the airfields rebuilt in the early days of Harris's control of Bomber Command. (David W. Fell and RAF Elsham Wolds Association)

At the time the entire front line strength of Bomber Command was just 600 aircraft, with another 350 bombers in training units. Harris intended to put all these aircraft in the skies, and to make up the number to 1,000 he called on Coastal Command, which refused to help, and the Army, which did join in with its ground attack aircraft. Fighter Command agreed to send out Spitfires and Hurricanes to attack German fighter bases at dusk.

Manufacturers were asked to rush forward deliveries, and pilots too elderly to fly operationally were asked to volunteer for this one mission. At Elsham Wolds, Group Captain Hugh Constantine gleefully accepted the chance to fly in combat for the first time in months. The crews had been aware for days that something special was planned, for routine missions had been curtailed to keep all aircraft in flying condition. When the crews at Scampton were told of the target and that over 1,000 aircraft were taking part they broke out in cheers. In all 1,047 aircraft took off on the evening of 30 May 1942, of which 970 were bombers heading for Cologne.

The bomber squadrons of Lincolnshire did, of course, put every aircraft that could fly into the air. Now based at Skellingthorpe, 50 Squadron launched 15 Manchesters one of which was flown by Flying Officer Leslie Manser. Born in India in 1922, Manser was educated in England and joined the RAF in August 1940. He joined 50 Squadron as an operational pilot a year later and by the time of the Thousand Bomber Raid on Cologne had completed several missions to Germany and occupied Europe.

As so often with the Manchester, Manser found he could not reach his supposed operating height of 17,000 feet and instead lumbered along at just 7,000 feet. The Manchester was still at this height as it entered the maelstrom in the skies above Cologne. Lining up on his bombing run, Manser had almost reached the target when a searchlight found the bomber. A second searchlight homed in, soon followed by the inevitable flak. Just after bomb-aimer Richard Barnes dropped the bombs, an anti-aircraft shell exploded inside the bomb bay. The doors of the bomb bay were torn off, the fuselage riddled with shrapnel and the rear gunner, B. Naylor, was wounded.

Manser put the aircraft into a diving turn to shake off the searchlights. A volley of 20 mm cannonfire raked the aircraft, starting a fire in the central fuselage. While the co-pilot, Sergeant L. Baveystock, tackled the flames, Manser struggled to get the damaged bomber up to 2,000 feet. With the fire out, the crew decided to head for Kent and began throwing out any loose equipment to save weight and so gain height. Then as the crew began to feel they would get home, the port engine exploded and fell silent.

Manser realised that the bomber was losing height rapidly, so he ordered the crew to bale out. It took some time to get the wounded Naylor out of the door, to be followed by all the crew except Baveystock. He dashed forward to report to Manser that the crew had gone and that it was time for him to bale out himself. Manser waved him aside shouting, 'For God's sake get out.'

Baveystock did so. He leapt clear into the darkness and pulled the ripcord of his parachute. But before the parachute had time to open, Baveystock plunged feet first into deep, freezing cold water. He struggled back to the surface to see the bomber hit the ground and explode less than a hundred yards away. Baveystock was relieved to find he had landed in a Dutch dyke rather than the North Sea and scrambled to firm ground.

Manser must have been aware of how low the aircraft was when he ordered the crew to bale out and that his own chances of getting out alive were slim indeed. He was awarded a posthumous Victoria Cross.

Issued in 1976, this First Day Cover commemorates the winning of the Victoria Cross by Flying Officer Leslie Manser of 50 Squadron.

With the exception of the navigator, who twisted his ankle on landing and was quickly caught by the Germans, the rest of the crew fled the crash site and made contact with the Dutch Resistance. They were smuggled across France and over the Pyrenees to reach Gibraltar. By October they were all back in England.

The Cologne raid was judged to be a success. Reconnaissance photos the next day revealed a breathtaking scene of devastation. One famous photo showed the dark bulk of Cologne Cathedral standing alone in a sea of rubble and ruins. After the war, German papers revealed that 12,840 buildings in Cologne were destroyed that night, making 45,132 people homeless – most of them industrial workers. In addition 328 factories had been flattened, an oil refinery destroyed and the rail system utterly annihilated. Although fewer than 500 people were killed, thanks to the well-constructed German air raid shelters, Cologne ceased to function as an industrial city for weeks afterwards.

Harris launched two more massive raids, on Essen and Bremen, in June. He then cancelled the massive 'Thousand Bomber Raids'. The effort was so great that other missions could not be flown, and losses among training crews were too high. He decided to opt for a pattern of smaller area attacks against the key industrial cities. Throughout the rest of 1942 and into 1943 Bomber Command was honing its skills.

The towers of Cologne Cathedral stand gaunt against the sky amid the ruins of the city centre in June 1945. Although it had been hit 15 times by bombs, the cathedral remained standing. The missing sections of roof and damaged walls were repaired within a few years of the end of the war.

One skill that would prove to be increasingly important as the months passed was a manoeuvre known as the 'corkscrew'. The ability to perform this complex stunt in a heavy bomber was notoriously difficult to acquire. Instructors frequently found it easier to show a trainee pilot how to do the corkscrew than attempt to describe on the ground the sequence of control changes needed. Essentially, the corkscrew saw the bomber twisting and turning as it performed a dive followed by a climb. The manoeuvre was designed to get the plane out of the beams of the German searchlights that enabled flak gunners or night-fighters to target their deadly fire on the illuminated bomber.

One man who perfected the corkscrew was Wing Commander William Abercromby. In July, Abercromby was flying a Manchester of 50 Squadron from Skellingthorpe on a raid over Dusseldorf. The bomber was caught by a searchlight, then three more zeroed in until Abercromby's aircraft was caught in a classic 'cone' of light. An ominous hail of machine gun fire announced that a German fighter was attacking, though little damage was inflicted. Abercromby threw the bomber into a corkscrew, evading the searchlights. As the bomber slipped into darkness the German fighter appeared in the dazzling glare of the concentrated beams. Abercromby's rear gunner at once opened fire, sending the German crashing to the ground.

For this, and a low-level daylight raid on Milan a few weeks later, Abercromby was awarded the DFC. Remarkably, Abercromby repeated his corkscrew trick when coned by searchlights over Berlin in December 1943 and received a bar to his DFC.

On the Dusseldorf raid when Abercromby evaded a cone of searchlights, Pilot Officer Leonard Jackson of 83 Squadron proved less lucky. Flying a Lancaster, Jackson was also 'coned'. Before he could even begin the corkscrew, Jackson's aircraft was hit twice by flak. First the starboard outer engine was knocked out, then the port outer engine took a direct hit and blew apart. The plane dived uncontrollably, turning to port, and this threw off the searchlights. But Jackson found he had dropped to 6,000 feet before he regained control and turned for home. Over the Dutch coast the Lancaster was again 'coned' and again hit by flak. Despite this damage, Jackson got his aircraft back to base and some weeks later was awarded a DFC.

Also in July 1942 a young Canadian by the name of Donald Curtin flew his Wellington on his very first combat mission, to bomb a target in Germany close to the Dutch border. It proved to be an eventful first outing.

As the aircraft approached the target area, it was attacked by a night-fighter. Throwing the bomber into a steep dive, Curtin escaped the stream of bullets and the enemy was seen no more. Getting back on course, Curtin reached the target rather behind the rest of the stream, dropped his bombs and turned for home. As the Wellington crossed the Dutch border it was again attacked, this time by three night-fighters at once. This disturbing change in German tactics proved effective. Curtin's aircraft was hit several times, while the rear gunner and wireless operator were both badly wounded.

Escaping the fighters, Curtin immediately came under anti-aircraft fire as his plane crossed the coast. A shell exploded in front of the cockpit, sending a piece of shrapnel into the navigator and temporarily blinding Curtin. Finally getting the burning cordite out of his eyes, Curtin realised the aircraft was now dangerously low over the sea and wallowing badly as its control surfaces were pierced in dozens of places.

Curtin nursed his Wellington over the coast, then belly-landed into an empty field. Having got his crew out of the wreckage, Curtin realised he was the least badly wounded man present, so he limped off to try to find a farmhouse in the blackout. After blundering around for over an hour, he managed to find help. Medical care was swift and all the crew survived. Curtin himself went on to fly numerous more missions with a new crew and in January 1943 won a bar to his DFC in action against more night-fighters, this time over Berlin.

In October 1942 Harris was able to announce that all bomber squadrons flying to Germany would soon receive new four-engined bombers. The men serving in Lincolnshire were particularly delighted to learn that they would all be getting Lancasters – which were already establishing a reputation as tough and reliable aircraft in combat. The changeover would, however, take time. It was 5 Group that completed the changeover first. The first squadron in 1 Group to receive Lancasters was 12 Squadron. But there was still one more mission to fly in the old Wellingtons. It was to Saarbrucken, a key industrial target in the southern Rhine area.

Among the men most keenly looking forward to the change of aircraft was Pilot Officer George Penrose, a rear gunner. The rear turret in the Lancaster was known to have a smoother, faster action than that in the Wellington and it boasted four machine guns instead of two. Before the night over Saarbrucken was finished he would wish he had those two extra guns.

The target was reached and bombed without incident, but on the return flight Penrose noticed the dark outline against the distant stars of another aircraft shadowing his own. He alerted his pilot over the intercom, but at first was not certain if the two-engined aircraft was another bomber or a night-fighter. He was left in no doubt when the interloper dived to attack. The bright flames of gunfire spurted from the nose of the other aircraft and Penrose returned fire enthusiastically.

This first attack produced no hits on either participant, but soon the German was climbing for position to repeat the assault. Again and again the German attacked, peppering the Wellington with holes but miraculously failing to hit anything vital. On the tenth pass, the German managed an accurate burst that struck Penrose's turret with unwelcome effect. The perspex canopy shattered into fragments, but Penrose was somehow uninjured and one of his guns was still working.

After several more attacks, the German again approached from the rear. This time Penrose hosed shots from his single remaining gun straight at the enemy, who returned fire with equal vigour. A sudden bang sounded from behind Penrose as a bullet smashed the turret gearing, jamming it solid. At almost the same instant a tongue of flame erupted from the enemy's port engine. The German plane turned over and dived towards the ground trailing flame behind it.

Perched alone in the freezing night air in a turret that no longer worked, Penrose gradually calmed down after the combat. Reasoning he could do very little that was constructive where he was, he clambered back into the body of the plane. The scene was a shambles. The entire fuselage was riddled with holes and both the navigator and wireless operator were wounded. Setting to work with the first aid box, Penrose cared for his comrades while the pilot got the damaged aircraft down on an emergency landing strip in southern England. Penrose was given a DFC for his night's work.

One lesson learned by Bomber Command in spectacular fashion was that the standard automatic pilot on the Lancaster had a serious flaw at high altitude. On the night of 28 November an Australian pilot, Ted Laing of 103 Squadron, was returning over the Alps from a raid on Turin. At 18,000 ft his Lancaster suddenly went into a steep dive, tipping right over to stand on its nose as it headed towards the snowy peaks below. Laing stood up, tugging at the control column to no effect. After diving for a

Australian pilot Ted Laing, photographed in Lincolnshire at the start of his combat career with Bomber Command. (David W. Fell and RAF Elsham Wolds Association)

few seconds, the aircraft then reared straight up and stood on its tail. All four engines cut out instantly and the aircraft fell back sickeningly towards the mountains. Almost unbelievably, Laing got the engines started and regained control. He then flew home without further mishap. It transpired that ice had caused the autopilot to cut in and perform the extraordinary manoeuvres in an attempt to get control away from the human pilot. Changes were made.

Laing and his crew went on to take part in another raid on Turin in December, when two engines cut out and Laing had to weave between the mountains on his way home. A mission to Essen was no less eventful in January 1943. The oxygen system developed a fault, which sent the rear

Ted Laing, photographed with his crew late in 1942, by which time they were seasoned veterans. (David W. Fell and RAF Elsham Wolds Association)

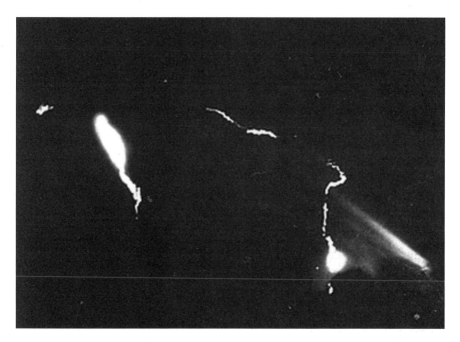

A remarkable photograph taken by a Dutch civilian living in Enschede, Holland, of Ted Laing's Lancaster crashing in flames. The main part of the burning aircraft is seen in the lower right of the picture. (David W. Fell and RAF Elsham Wolds Association)

gunner and bomber to sleep before Laing realised the cause of his own drowsiness and dived to lower altitude. The Lancaster was hit by flak during a raid on Berlin on 16 January, but Laing and his crew were back in the air on 21 January for another raid on Essen. The aircraft was shot down over Enschede, Holland, and there were no survivors.

In December 1942 a Lancaster of 50 Squadron from Skellingthorpe was returning from a raid over Germany when a flak shell exploded close behind the cockpit. The wireless operator was killed outright, while pilot Roy Calvert received a large piece of shrapnel in his left arm and navigator John Medani was hit twice in the back. The front gunner scrambled out of his turret to administer first aid to the wounded men. Medani was worst hit and was rapidly losing blood. Nevertheless, he insisted on working on his charts to produce a direct course home to Lincolnshire. Handing the crucial piece of paper to Calvert, he fainted. With the gunner helping move the flight column, Calvert got the bomber back intact. He was given a DFC, while Medani got a much-deserved Distinguished Flying Medal (DFM).

In March 1943 Harris decided it was time to mount a major new bombing offensive. This would not be a repeat of the Thousand Bomber Raids, but a sustained assault by smaller formations of heavy bombers, designed to grind down an area with prolonged bombardment. The area Harris chose was the Ruhr, the industrial heart of Germany. The densely-packed industrial complex flanked the Ruhr river where it flowed into the Rhine. The whole region was protected by flak, night-fighters and searchlights, but Harris believed his command was up to the challenge. On 5 March the assault began with 442 bombers heading for Essen.

One man who started his flying career with the RAF in this Battle of the Ruhr was the extraordinary Florent Victor Paul Van Rolleghem. He had been a pilot in the Belgian Air Force, but was captured when the Germans overran his native Belgium. When Van Rolleghem was released in February 1941 he decided that his flying skills would be more use in Britain than in Brussels, so he walked across France, over the Pyrenees, through Spain and into Portugal. There he presented himself as a dishevelled figure speaking no English to the British Consulate in Lisbon and asked to join the RAF.

By July he was in England and in April 1943 was posted to 103 Squadron

The Belgian pilot Florent Victor Paul Van Rolleghem poses with his first crew on the tail of their Lancaster. All except Van Rolleghem were killed a few weeks later. (David W. Fell and RAF Elsham Wolds Association)

Van Rolleghem and three of his second crew recreate the pose for a later photograph. (David W. Fell and RAF Elsham Wolds Association)

at Elsham Wolds. Van Rolleghem proved himself to be an exceptional pilot and was hugely popular with his squadron. On 24 July he was awarded a Distinguished Flying Cross for nursing his crippled aircraft back to base, a feat he repeated three times in missions over the Ruhr. By this time Van Rolleghem was reckoned to be a hero by the Air Ministry, who decided to use his flair for the dramatic on a lecture tour of factories in Britain.

Now promoted to Acting Squadron Leader, he was posted back to

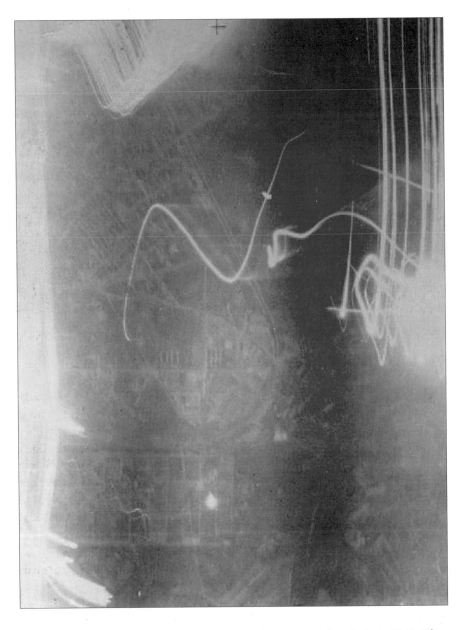

A photo taken by Van Rolleghem of 103 Squadron on a raid to Turin in 1943. The streets of the city can just be made out behind the bright flares. (David W. Fell and RAF Elsham Wolds Association)

Florent Victor Paul Van Rolleghem gathered together his air and ground crews for this photograph. (David W. Fell and RAF Elsham Wolds Association)

Elsham Wolds to join 103 Squadron in March 1944. He then fell seriously ill, and was devastated when his crew was shot down while flying with a replacement pilot. He talked the station Medical Officer into changing his designation of 'Unfit to Fly' to 'Unfit to Fly at High Altitude' and went back to war. He completed his second tour on 3 August 1944 and immediately started a third tour with the same crew. This was completed on 26 October 1944. On 22 October 1944 he was awarded a well-earned and overdue Distinguished Service Order. He had flown 70 operations in 18 months – not once did he fail to bomb his target.

After the war, Van Rolleghem rejoined the Belgian Air Force, rising to the rank of Air Marshal of the Belgian Air Force before his retirement in January 1970.

Early in April Flight Lieutenant Kenneth Bickers was piloting his Halifax on a raid against Duisburg in the Ruhr. The bombing was completed uneventfully, but on the return journey a twin-engined night-fighter dived out of the dark and opened fire. The devastating first fusillade killed the rear gunner outright and severely wounded the upper gunner, as well as

A Handley Page Halifax, its squadron identification letters obscured by the censor, flies in low over Lincolnshire.

starting a fire in the rear of the fuselage.

Recovering from his shock, Bickers saw the German climb up in front of the Halifax and circle overhead, obviously waiting to see what would happen. While the wireless operator tackled the flames with an extinguisher, the German came down for a second attack. Bickers threw the Halifax into evasive action, but the German bullets riddled the port wing, puncturing the fuel tank. A third attack saw a hail of shot plough into the wireless operator's empty position, smashing all his equipment. The hydraulic system was destroyed and the elevator control cables cut through.

The Halifax lurched dangerously and entered a dive. It took Bickers some time to regain control, by which time the German had gone – perhaps believing he had shot his enemy down. Bickers nursed the badly damaged bomber across the North Sea to reach East Anglia. Arriving over an airfield, Bickers realised that the gunner was too badly injured to bale out. He then

A German soldier stands guard while a workman inspects a gun recovered from the wreckage of Mooney's bomber the day after it crashed. (David W. Fell and RAF Elsham Wolds Association)

Pilot Officer J.O.B. Mooney, photographed when a Flight Sergeant. A volunteer from New Zealand, he was killed on one of his first missions over Germany. (David W. Fell and RAF Elsham Wolds Association)

put the aircraft down in a nerve-racking crash-landing, which saved the lives of his wounded crewmate and won him a DFC.

Although most of Bomber Command's efforts were concentrated on the Ruhr at this time, other targets were hit. On 16 April 103 Squadron was sent to attack the Skoda Works in Pilsen, Czechoslovakia, which the Germans were using to manufacture armoured vehicles.

Flying on the mission was Pilot Officer J.O.B. Mooney who had volunteered in his native New Zealand. After pilot training and a stint at an Operational Training Unit, Mooney came to 103 Squadron. The mission to Pilsen did not go well and just after midnight Mooney's aircraft was hit by anti-aircraft fire over Ludwigshafen am Rhein. Mooney ordered his crew to bale out as he wrestled with the controls of the doomed aircraft. Sergeant Biggs and Sergeant Rouse baled out, but the Lancaster was by this point hurtling towards the ground streaming flames and smoke. None of the other crew members escaped, but Mooney did steer the aircraft

Bill Donnahey, photographed in civilian clothing. At this date all aircrew carried such photos when flying over enemy territory. The photos were designed so that they could be used on false ID documents if the man was shot down and was then lucky enough to make contact with the Resistance. (David W. Fell and RAF Elsham Wolds Association)

Bill Donnahey, the champion air gunner of 199 Squadron, was much in demand to fill in for sick colleagues among the crews of the squadron. He completed his first tour in a surprisingly short time. (David W. Fell and RAF Elsham Wolds Association)

straight into a German flak battery. The resulting explosions utterly destroyed the German guns and their crews.

On the night of 20 April the Wellingtons of 199 Squadron took off from Ingham on a 'gardening' mission to lay mines off the French port of Lorient. Laying mines was a difficult task that involved flying low over the sea in a precise pattern, dropping the mines at prescribed intervals. The Luftwaffe night-fighter pilots soon got

Bill Donnahey's wedding was held in 1944. Various members of the two families pooled their precious clothing ration stamps so that the happy couple and their attendants could be suitably dressed for the occasion. (David W. Fell and RAF Elsham Wolds Association)

The badge of 57 Squadron. Although a pre-war bomber squadron this formation did not move to Lincolnshire until the summer of 1943.

to know the pattern followed by minelayers and could manoeuvre their aircraft into a good attacking position. As the Wellington flown by Pilot Officer Archer was nearing the end of its pattern, a Junkers 88 night-fighter pounced. Rear gunner Bill Donnahey reacted quickly, pouring fire into the approaching German aircraft. The attacker veered off and dived out of sight. Donnahey's reputation as an air gunner was made and he was always much in demand both at 199 and later with 103 Squadron where he completed his second tour of operations. He survived the war.

On 13 May 57 Squadron took off from Scampton to attack a motor works. On the return journey the Lancaster flown by Pilot Officer Jan Haye was shot down over Ensched in the Netherlands. Haye, a Dutch airman who had fled to Britain when the Netherlands was overrun in May 1940, landed uninjured, but could not find his crew. He learned later that two had died and the rest had been arrested by the Germans soon after they landed.

Haye dumped his flying gear and RAF jacket before setting off to try to find help. Unknown to him, the Germans had recently arrested a number of locals for aiding downed RAF crew. Although the farmers he approached would not take him in, they did give him food and a bike to help him get to his own home town, Hilversum. At Apeldoorn, Haye cycled past a column of German infantry, none of whom gave him a second glance. Eventually Haye made contact with a man he had known before the war and whom he guessed would be actively anti-German. The man was not involved with the Resistance, but told Haye to go to The Hague and make contact with a government official named Anton Schrader, who was.

Having met Schrader, Haye was whisked off to a safe house in The Hague, where he stayed hidden for the next two months. Schrader was in charge of organising coastal barges carrying food from farms to towns and cities. He had arranged for one barge to be secretly converted to carry a hidden boat that was used for various Resistance missions. Interesting as this was, Haye was more taken with Elly de Jong, the young woman in whose house he was hiding.

On 26 July Schrader took Haye to the docks where he boarded the converted barge to meet another downed RAF pilot and several Dutchmen who were wanted by the Germans. That night the men were launched into the North Sea from the barge, aboard a small rowing boat with some food and a sail. After a voyage of four days and nights they were picked up by a Royal Navy destroyer in the Thames Estuary.

Haye returned to his squadron, subsequently transferring to the Pathfinders and winning a DFC for a later flight. As soon as Germany surrendered, Haye asked for leave and for permission to travel to Holland. He found that both Schrader and Elly de Jong had been arrested by the Gestapo in 1943 and held in concentration camps. Remarkably both survived and that autumn Haye married Elly. They lived to celebrate their Golden Wedding Anniversary in 1997.

Harris called off the Battle of the Ruhr at the end of July 1943. By that time most of the region lay in ruins and industrial output had been seriously reduced. Some areas suffered worse than others. The small iron-smelting town of Remscheid had 80% of its buildings destroyed and 90% of its output halted. Even by October the town was producing only half the iron it had in January. The Germans were soon moving industrial works out of the Ruhr and dispersing them, and their workers, to other towns and cities. Harris sent Bomber Command to follow them.

But before Bomber Command turned its attentions away from the Ruhr, there was one vital set of targets that had to be destroyed to ensure that the area could not regain its industrial output. It was time for the most famous raid of the entire war, and it was to be flown from Lincolnshire.

It was time for the Dambusters.

Handley Page Halifax

Type:	Heavy bomber
Engines:	Mk I–V 4 x 1,460 hp
	Rolls-Royce Merlin X
	Mk VI–IX 4 x 1,800 hp
	Bristol Hercules 100
Wingspan:	98 ft 10 in
Length:	70 ft 1 in
Height:	20 ft 9 in
Weight:	Empty 33,860 lb
	Loaded 65,000 lb
Armament:	Mk I–V 8 x 0.303 in machine guns in nose and tail turrets and beam windows
	Mk VI–IX 8 x 0.303 in machine guns in dorsal and tail turrets and ventral opening
Bombload:	13,000 lb
Max speed:	265 mph
Ceiling:	18,000 ft
Range:	2,400 miles
Production:	6,176

It was in 1937 that Handley Page began work on a four-engined bomber to replace the Hampden, which was then its main production bomber aircraft. The Halifax proved to be a dependable and versatile aircraft, which flew with Coastal Command as well as Bomber Command. The roomy fuselage proved especially useful for variants, such as its role as paratroop transport and cargo aircraft and for electronic countermeasures.

Chapter 6

The Dambusters Raid

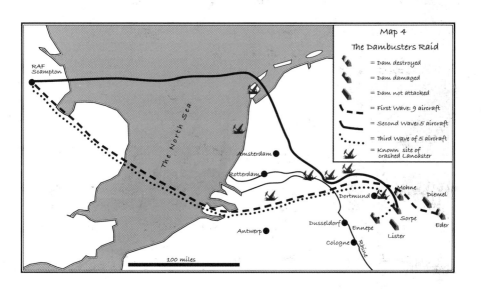

The chain of events that led up to the famous Dambusters Raid began the day before war was declared. Aircraft designer Barnes Wallis, who had designed the Wellington bomber for Vickers, decided to search for a way in which bombers could cripple Germany's industrial might and so shorten the war. He quickly came to the conclusion that this could best be achieved by destroying either the sources of power or the means of transport. He turned to power first.

The Romanian oilfields were too distant for bombers to reach from Britain and coal mines were too deep underground to be affected by bombs. That left dams. Germany was fortunate in having mountainous regions close to her industrial centres. These mountains had high rainfall and deep valleys, which made them ideal for building dams. These dams provided hydro-electric power, but they also stored the vast quantities of water needed by the heavy industry of the 1940s and they were often used as reservoirs for the canal system as well. Destroy a dam, reasoned Wallis, and you could badly hit power, industry and transport in one go.

There were three dams that stood out as being key to Germany's industry, all of them in the range of hills between the Rhine and Ruhr rivers. The Möhne Dam held 134 million tons of water. The Eder held 212 million tons of water and also fed water into the Mittelland Canal, Germany's busiest industrial waterway. The Sorpe held around 180 million tons of water and fed drinking water to the surrounding cities. Together the three provided nearly half the electric power of the vast Ruhr industrial metropolis.

That the destruction of the dams would be a huge blow to Germany, nobody could doubt. The question was how to go about destroying them.

Dams are, by their very nature, enormously strong structures. They are also long and narrow targets to try to hit with bombs from the air. Wallis knew that even the largest bomb then in existence would barely scratch the surface of one of the massive concrete structures, even if a bomb-aimer could hit it.

The lines of Wallis's thoughts thus far had been followed by others. The RAF had considered the dams as a target, but then discarded the idea as being impossible to carry out from the air. The Germans concluded much the same, so they put only light defences at the dams.

But Wallis was not deterred. As an engineer he knew that the concrete dams were strong, but brittle. If he could find a way to shake the dams with enough force they would shatter to pieces. After months of work he realised that the key was to generate shockwaves. This could best be done by pressing a concentrated charge against the wall of the dam about 50 feet below the surface of the water. This position would mean that the shockwaves from the explosion would be reflected back by the weight of the water into the concrete of the dam. In turn this would shake the dam with great force, shattering the concrete.

The next problem was how to position a charge so precisely. Sabotage was out of the question in the heart of Germany, so only a bomb could do the work. However, no known bomb could be dropped accurately enough to reach a position under water. Wallis went to work once again.

It was not until 1942 that Wallis, working in his spare time, came up with the answer. He found that putting a drum-shaped bomb against a dam wall and letting it sink into the water would ensure it remained pressed against the wall if it was first given a moderate backspin. He also knew that a round object given backspin would skip on water, rather like a flat stone thrown by children on a beach. Putting the two together, Wallis came up with his revolutionary 'Bouncing Bomb'.

The bomb was to be drum-shaped and dropped from an aircraft flying low over the water. A mechanism would give the bomb backspin as it dropped, making it bounce off the water surface until it hit the dam wall. The wall would stop the bomb, but the backspin would continue as it sank to keep it pressed against the dam. The theory was sound, but engineering difficulties remained and to solve them Wallis needed to build and test half-size bomb models.

In December 1942 Wallis used his contacts to get a test bomb built and borrowed a Wellington to drop it – as Wallis himself said when asking for the aircraft, 'I designed it.' The first test drops went awry, but Wallis persisted and by February 1943 he had a fully working half-size bouncing bomb. The lakes behind the dams would be at their fullest after the winter rains in April or May, so that would be the best time to destroy them.

A meeting with Arthur Harris was arranged by Mutt Summers, a senior figure at Vickers who had known the head of Bomber Command for years. The meeting began with Harris in typically combative mood. As soon as Wallis entered the office, and before he could unpack his briefcase, Harris demanded, 'What the hell is it you want? My boys' lives are too precious to be wasted on your crazy notions.'

Unabashed, Wallis produced his facts and figures, his drawings and films of his models. After a lengthy meeting and a barrage of questions, all of which Wallis was able to answer, Harris leaned back in his chair. 'So you really think you can knock a dam down with that thing?' he demanded.

'Yes,' said Wallis. 'Well, three or four probably.'

'Fine,' returned Harris. 'But if you think you can just walk in here and get a squadron of Lancasters out of me you've made a mistake.'

'I don't want a squadron,' replied Wallis. 'Just one Lancaster to prove to you it will work.'

'Do that,' concluded Harris, 'and I'll give you a squadron.' Then he signalled Wallis and Summers to leave.

With Harris's support, Wallis suddenly found he had every engineering facility he could wish for. With an army of skilled workers he was able to produce the finished bomb in weeks. This turned out to be 7 feet across and rather longer than expected. Roy Chadwick, head of engineering at Avro, was tasked with fitting the bomb and its spinning mechanism inside a Lancaster. He found the only way to achieve this was to remove the bomb bay doors and the upper turret.

Wallis, meanwhile, was finding that making a real bomb work was rather different from producing a half-scale replica. The bomb would need to be dropped from a height of 60 feet and at a precise speed when exactly the right distance from the dam. The raid was going to call for exceptional flying abilities as well as great courage.

Harris, meanwhile, had thought much the same thing. As with the Augsburg Raid, he turned at once to his old command, 5 Group in Lincolnshire. He sent for Air Vice Marshal Ralph Cochrane, Commander of the Group, and announced, 'I've got a job for you Cocky.' He then told Cochrane to find Guy Gibson, who had been in 5 Group since the outbreak of war, and appoint him to command a new squadron formed especially for this one mission. Together Cochrane and Gibson were to choose crews able to fly low at night, then train them rigorously for the dambusting attack.

In all 21 crews, 147 men were chosen and on 21 March the newly formed 617 Squadron assembled at Scampton. At once they were given the task of flying cross country at night at low level, on routes that took them again and again over lakes. Gibson, like all his men, knew nothing about the mission and puzzled over these strange orders. Not until 15 April was Gibson told of the target, but this was only so that he could arrange more meaningful training and he was forbidden to tell his squadron.

On 6 May the converted Lancasters arrived at Scampton, without the bombs, and the squadron began its final preparations. The problems of

One of the finest and most famous war movies ever made celebrated the Dambusters Raid. This photograph, signed by star Richard Todd, shows him in his role as Guy Gibson.

bomb aiming had been solved. The task of flying at exactly 60 feet above water at night was accomplished by placing a searchlight in the nose of each aircraft and another in the tail. These were angled down beneath the bomber so that they crossed exactly 60 feet below the aircraft. The bomb-aimer would watch the lights on the water, directing the pilot to climb or dive until the lights crossed.

Even simpler was the solution to the problem of dropping the bomb the correct distance from the dam. Each dam had two towers located on its parapet to hold control and pumping equipment. Each bomb-aimer had an uncomplicated wooden triangle with pegs set in it in such a way that when the pegs lined up on the towers, the bomber was in the correct place for the bomb to be dropped. The distance was crucial. If the bomb were dropped too soon it would sink away from the dam and be useless. If it were dropped too late it might bounce over the dam completely.

Weather forecasts predicted that the night of 16 May would be ideal for the raid. Wallis travelled to Scampton for the briefing so as to be on hand to answer questions from the crews. Only then did the crews learn where they were going and the purpose of the arduous training. As soon as the briefing was over and Wallis had left, the gates to Scampton were locked. Nobody was going in or out until the raid was over. Secrecy was paramount.

A few hours later a lone car arrived at 5 Group HQ at Grantham. The guard stopped it to peer into the vehicle, then hastily snapped to attention. Arthur Harris had arrived to be with Cochrane and Wallis at the radio receiver. Together they would hear the news as it came in from the aircraft over the dams.

There was one casualty even before the aircraft took off. Gibson's beloved pet dog, Nigger, was run over and killed. Gibson decided to use the word 'Nigger' as the codeword for the destruction of the Möhne Dam in tribute. He asked a colleague to bury the dog outside his office at the precise time he was due to be leading the bombers into the attack. If things went badly, both man and dog would be going into the ground at the same time.

At 21.25 that evening the Lancaster engines roared into life. The Dambusters Raid had begun.

The squadron was flying in three waves. Leading the first wave was Guy Gibson in the aircraft codemarked 'G George', which he always insisted on using, if at all possible, in whatever squadron he served. With him flew eight other Lancasters – piloted by John Hopgood and Michael Martin in the front formation, followed ten minutes later by 'Dinghy' Young, Astell and David Maltby, then another ten minutes passed before Henry Maudslay, Knight and David Shannon took off. This first wave was detailed to attack the Möhne Dam, then, if that was successfully destroyed, to move on to the Eder.

The second wave was made up of five Lancasters – piloted by Joe McCarthy, Byers, Barlow, Geoff Rice and Les Munro. Their task was twofold: to fly on a northern route to divert German night-fighters and then to attack the Sorpe Dam. The third wave was to be made up of aircraft piloted by Townsend, Brown, Anderson, Ottley and Burpee. They were to act as a mobile reserve, called up to attack whichever target was deemed most suitable on the night.

The flight out took one hour and ten minutes. The aircraft flew as low as they dared to avoid enemy radar and flak. As they crossed the Dutch coast, German searchlights probed the darkness to find the source of the engine noise. When they found the Lancasters, flak guns opened fire. Munro's aircraft was hit and he turned for home. More dramatically, Rice's Lancaster was so low it hit the water of the Zuyder Zee. His bomb was torn

Another photo taken on the set of The Dambusters *movie and signed by actor Richard Todd, shows the view from Gibson's Lancaster as it approaches the Möhne Dam.*

from the fuselage and the rear turret was buried in ice cold seawater. The rear gunner feared he would drown, but the water sloshed out as fast as it had come. Rice, too, turned for base. A flak shell hit Barlow's aircraft, setting off the mighty bouncing bomb. The resulting blast flared as bright as the sun for a second, then died. No trace of the bomber was ever found. A little while later Byers was also shot down.

The survivors were now racing across the dark landscape as low as their long hours of practice would let them dare. At one point, Gibson, Martin and Hopgood had to climb rapidly to avoid a line of power cables. Another incident came when Young almost hit a house, not realising he was so low until it was almost too late. Astell did not make it, crashing for some unknown reason during this manic low-level chase across the dark landscape of blacked out Europe.

A little before midnight they arrived over the dams. The first wave found the Möhne without much trouble. The ten guns around the dam were flaming tracer into the sky as soon as the sound of Lancaster engines thundered down from above. Gibson radioed his aircraft: 'Hello. I am going in to attack. Hello 'M Mother'. Stand by to take over if anything happens.'

Hopgood, the pilot of M Mother and designated to take over if Gibson died, replied quickly: 'Good Luck.'

G George banked over the far end of the Möhne lake, then dropped down low as the engines roared to take the bomber up to 240 mph. Gibson aimed the bomber straight between the towers some three miles distant, dropped down to what he thought was about the right height and flicked on the searchlights that would tell his bomb-aimer their precise height. As soon as the lights came on, the German gunners could see the bomber as clearly as if it were day. A stream of tracer lanced out from each dam tower, flak shells coming from the shores adding to the lethal shower of fire.

Gibson flinched as a sudden noise erupted, but it was only Deering, his front gunner, opening fire on the dam towers. Tracer bullets were now flying in both directions, tearing fire red across the sky. Then the bomb was gone, seconds later the aircraft was over the dam, almost scraping the concrete ridge as it dived away from the German guns. Gibson dived down into the blackness of the valley while his rear gunner hosed bullets at the enemy, then he pulled the Lancaster back into the sky and looked over his shoulder.

A vast column of water a thousand feet high soared into the sky as the

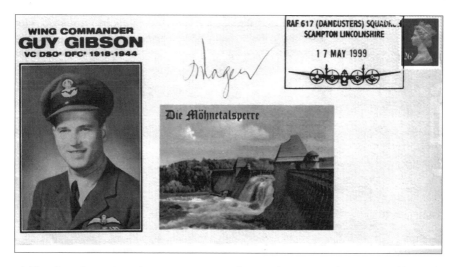

A First Day Cover issued to commemorate the Dambusters Raid. It is signed by Jack Hager DFC, a Flight Lieutenant with 617 Squadron.

bouncing bomb exploded. The white water crashed back down to the lake, but the dam held. For some minutes the lake surface writhed and boiled, then calmed. Gibson sent Hopgood in second.

Hopgood made a perfect run, but just before the spot where he was due to drop his bomb something went wrong. The aircraft was seen to veer left, then fire erupted from the port wing. The bomb was dropped late, bouncing over the dam and exploding in the valley beyond. The Lancaster was climbing away from the target when it exploded in a fireball.

Martin, flying P Popsie, was third to attack. This time Gibson dived at the dam just as Martin was beginning his run. The tracer fired by Gibson's gunners distracted the men on the dam so the attacking Lancaster was halfway along the lake before it was spotted. The bomb fell precisely in the right spot and exploded beside the dam. Again the lake boiled, but again the dam was intact.

Fourth to attack was 'Dinghy' Young in A Apple. This time both Gibson and Martin dived on the dam with guns blazing to distract the defenders. Again the trick worked and Young made a perfect run. Maltby attacked next, those aircraft that had already attacked flying beside his down the lake with their lights on and guns firing to divert the defensive fire. It was another direct hit, but again the stubborn Möhne Dam stayed standing.

The Möhne Dam as it is today. The central area, where the dambusters blew a yawning gap in the dam, is clearly marked by different coloured facing stones.

Gibson called Shannon and told him to begin his run.

As Shannon's Lancaster came down to begin its attack, Martin's voice suddenly broke the radio silence. 'Hell! It's gone. It's gone. Look at it for Christ's sake.' There was no need to doubt what he was talking about. A jagged hole some 100 yards across and 100 feet deep had opened up in the dam. Water was pouring through the hole as a foaming, boiling avalanche. The jetstream of water was pushed over 200 feet through the air by the pressure of the lake behind before it hit the valley floor.

By the light of the moon the bomber crews watched as the awesome wall of liquid destruction poured down the valley. The flood was 25 feet high as it raced downhill at a staggering 20 feet per second. The first building to be destroyed was the hydro-electric power station below the dam, engulfed in seconds. Gibson's aircraft sent back the codeword 'Nigger'.

Back at Grantham the codeword was received with jubilation. Unaware of the casualties, Wallis threw his arms in the air and ran around the room. Harris stopped him and shook his hand. 'Wallis,' he said, 'I didn't believe a word you said about this damn bomb at first, but you could sell me a pink elephant now.' Cochrane just grinned.

Seconds later, Harris went off to inform his superior officer, Portal, of the success. Portal was, that evening, dining with US President Roosevelt in Washington. 'Get me the White House,' barked Harris at the telephone operator outside the control room. Not knowing about the raid and not recognising the officer talking to her, the WAAF operator put him through to the only 'White House' that any officer had ever asked for before: a pub

The North Tower on the Möhne Dam, photographed in 2005. Heavy machine guns mounted on the two towers formed the main anti-aircraft defence on the night of the raid.

on the road towards RAF Bottesford. It took over an hour to sort out the confusion.

Meanwhile, high above the turmoil, Gibson ordered Martin and Maltby to head back to Scampton. He led Young, Shannon, Maudslay and Knight off through the dark night towards the Eder Dam. Fog was drifting through the valleys and it was some time before he was certain they were in the right place. Having identified the lake and dam, Gibson called up David Shannon to begin his attack.

The Eder was more difficult to reach than the Möhne as the surrounding hills crowded in on the lake, restricting the approach run that the Lancasters could make. There were, however, no anti-aircraft guns. Five times Shannon made his run, and five times he pulled out. Gibson told him to take a break and sent Maudslay in Z Zebra to attack. The bomb was dropped and skipped over the water, but something went wrong. Instead of hitting the dam and sinking, it exploded as it struck the parapet. For an instant the Lancaster was outlined against the flash, then it was enveloped in flame and smoke.

'Hello Z Zebra,' radioed Gibson, more from a sense of duty than hoping to get a response, 'are you all right?'

There was only static. Then Maudslay's voice crackled over the airwaves: 'Yes. I think so. Stand by.' He was never heard from again and nobody can really explain what happened.

Shannon went in again next, was unhappy with his run and went around again. The bomb exploded directly in place, sending the by now familiar column of water climbing into the sky. But the dam held.

Only Knight was left to attack now and Gibson sent him in. After three failed runs, Shannon decided to take a hand. He talked Knight in and this time the bomb was dropped perfectly. The blast came, and the water soared upward. As Gibson watched he saw the wall of the dam seem to shiver, then a crack spread across its face and it collapsed. The torrent of water was this time even more spectacular than at the Möhne. There was more pressure forcing the avalanche through a narrower gap. The watching bomber crews saw a car in the valley, its dim headlights momentarily turning green as the waters enveloped it, then all was darkness.

Of the second wave, only the aircraft piloted by Joe McCarthy survived to reach Sorpe. He made a trial run, then went in to drop his bomb. Unlike the Möhne and Eder dams, the Sorpe was of composite earth and concrete construction. Wallis was not so certain his bombs would destroy it. In the event McCarthy's bomb shattered the upper sections of the dam, but failed to demolish it completely.

Of the third wave, the mobile reserve, Burpee had already been shot down. Brown was sent to attack the Sorpe, but when he arrived dense mist sat on the waters and his bomb-aimer found it impossible to focus the searchlights on the water surface. Finally he took a chance and dropped the bomb by guesswork, managing to hit the dam and causing more damage, but again not collapsing the structure.

Anderson was also sent to the Sorpe, but by the time he arrived the mist was so dense he could see nothing. He turned for home. Ottley was sent to the Lister Dam, but was shot down before he reached it. The final dambuster aircraft to be sent to the attack was Townsend flying O Orange. He found the Ennepe and made a perfect attack. The bomb exploded, but only light damage could be seen.

On the journey home Gibson evaded a night-fighter only by flying so low that he almost hit a cow, while Young was hit by flak and ditched in the North Sea. The survivors landed back at Scampton soon after dawn. Maltby was first back, and Townsend the last. Fifty-six men had not survived the raid. It was an appallingly high loss, almost half of those who had taken part. Wallis was devastated and Harris looked grim.

In Germany the damage inflicted was terrible. For 50 miles downstream from both the Möhne and Eder devastation was absolute. Factories and houses had been swept away by the torrent while coal mines were flooded and destroyed. Around 6,000 acres of farmland had been stripped of their crops and 6,500 cattle and pigs killed, while 25 bridges had been destroyed and hundreds of miles of road and rail swept away. The official German report listed 1,294 people as having been killed. Sadly, most of them were Russian prisoners of war who, unknown to the RAF, had been in a camp just below the Eder. In the Ruhr the lack of power and water caused a loss of production in the war industries that was officially estimated to be the equivalent of 500,000 man-months of work.

The Germans at once set to work repairing the damage. First they ringed the surviving dams with heavy anti-aircraft defences, then installed more around the wreckage to protect the repair workers. In all, 1,250 soldiers and 4,000 labourers were involved, taking them away from other war work and again affecting Germany's industries.

The cost of the raid to Bomber Command had been heavy, but the damage it inflicted was heavier still.

The memorial to 617 Squadron at Woodhall Spa takes the form of a stylised dam through which waters are bursting. The names of men killed serving with the squadron are engraved on the dam walls.
(http://www.oldairfields.fotopic.net/)

A few days later Gibson was told he had been awarded a Victoria Cross for his actions on the raid. Martin, McCarthy, Maltby, Shannon and Knight were given Distinguished Service Orders, while 14 officers were given DFCs and 12 men were awarded the DFM. Two, Brown and Townsend, got the Conspicuous Gallantry Medal (CGM).

Gibson was also told that 617 Squadron, now universally dubbed 'The Dambusters', was being made a permanent squadron to be tasked with missions calling for precision bombing. He drew up a number of designs for a new squadron badge and was trying to decide which to choose when

Scampton received a visit from King George VI. Gibson showed the King the sketches and asked his opinion. The King called over Queen Elizabeth, later the Queen Mother, and together they chose a picture showing a dam being struck by three bolts of lightning and with water pouring through the breach. The motto that went with it was 'Après Nous Le Deluge', a play on a famous quote from the French king Louis XV which translates as 'After us the flood'.

It became the squadron badge and is still used by 617 Squadron as the RAF enters the 21st century.

The propeller from a wrecked 617 Squadron Lancaster stands forlornly at their base, Woodhall Spa, to which the squadron moved from Scampton after the Dambusters Raid.
(http://www.oldairfields.fotopic.net/)

Chapter 7

From Lincolnshire to Germany

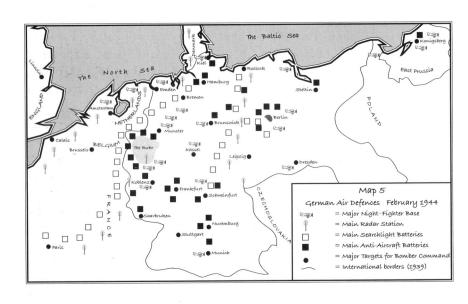

Map 5

German Air Defences February 1944

= Major Night-Fighter Base
= Main Radar Station
= Main Searchlight Batteries
= Main Anti-Aircraft Batteries
= Major Targets for Bomber Command
= International borders (1939)

By the time the Battle of the Ruhr came to an end in the summer of 1943, the nocturnal battles in the skies over Germany were changing rapidly as new equipment and new tactics came into operation.

For the men flying from Lincolnshire, the conversion to Lancasters from two-engined bombers or from Stirlings was rapidly reaching completion. They were also acquiring important aids to navigation. The 'Oboe' system enabled a navigator to plot his approximate position over western Germany. The much newer 'H2S' radar was very different. It scanned the ground ahead of the bomber to produce a rough, but accurate image of hills, mountains, built up areas and stretches of water. Using Oboe to get into position for an attack, then H2S to zero in on a target, a Lancaster could drop its bombs with some degree of accuracy at night. At first only a few bombers could be supplied with both sets of equipment. They acted as 'Pathfinders', dropping coloured flares to mark the target for the main stream of bombers following behind.

The Germans, too, were improving their defences. The number and accuracy of anti-aircraft guns around important targets was increased dramatically. By 1943 the gunners were assisted by searchlight batteries that had short-range radar sets to show them where the bombers were in the sky. A master blue-coloured searchlight was aimed at the radar plot, allowing the other searchlights to weave around, searching the correct area of sky to pick up a bomber.

But it was the night-fighters that were rapidly proving to be the most deadly of Germany's defences. From 1940 through to the end of the war, Bomber Command estimated it lost about 1% of aircraft on a raid to flak. But night-fighters were very different. In 1940 there were very few German fighters in the skies at night. Those that did appear were simply day-fighters patrolling the skies over potential targets in hope of spotting a bomber by moonlight. By the winter of 1941 the situation had changed as the Germans introduced new aircraft and tactics.

Leading the way in night-fighter design were Junkers with their Ju88C and Messerschmitt with their Bf110G. The designs of both aircraft were based on those of pre-war fighter-bombers that had proved less than successful in daylight aerial combat against the more nimble single-seat Spitfires and Hurricanes. Both aircraft had two engines and carried three crew members. They were large enough to hold airborne radar sets and the men to operate them, but agile enough to overtake bombers and attack them with deadly precision.

The Ju88C entered service in 1942 and some 3,200 were built over the next 18 months. The Bf110G began fighting a few months later but soon overtook the Junkers in terms of numbers, with an impressive 1,580 entering service in 1943 alone. Both aircraft were fitted with twin 20 mm cannon and two 7.9 mm machine guns firing forward, while the Bf110G had a pair of machine guns in the rear cockpit as well.

In 1943 both German night-fighter models gained a destructive new weapon in the shape of the 'schragmusik', or 'harsh music', a twin 20 mm cannon mounted to fire directly upwards. This enabled the German to approach a bomber by flying on the same course, but beneath it – thus largely avoiding the risk of being seen and keeping the fighter out of reach of the bomber's defensive guns. The German would then open fire, sending a stream of cannon shells tearing into the British aircraft's belly.

On 23 November 1943 a Lancaster from 207 Squadron received a devastating burst of fire from a schragmusik cannon. The shells struck the full bombload of incendiaries, which promptly caught fire. Only the quick action of Pilot Officer Pryor, who at once jettisoned the bombs, saved the aircraft.

To combat the German advances, the RAF developed their own electronic countermeasures. Obsolete Boulton Paul Defiant fighters were loaded with a radar jamming device codenamed 'Mandrel' and sent to fly with the bombers for the first leg of their journey. Other devices included powerful radio transmitters, which could be set to the same frequency as the German radios to block out any instructions from ground radar stations, and 'Boozer', which warned a bomber when it was being tracked by German radar. Each development led to a temporary dip in losses to night-fighters, but the Germans always found an answer within a few weeks.

Meanwhile, the men of 1 Group and 5 Group continued to fly their missions. They were being sent against industrial towns and cities across Germany with the aim of destroying factories, flattening housing districts and disrupting industrial output. But there was one sudden priority given to Harris that proved to be a highly productive distraction from the main business of the war.

On 25 July the Italian dictator Benito Mussolini had been ousted from power by the Grand Council of his own Fascist Party. Nobody on the Allied side was in any doubt that the move had come about because of Italian losses in North Africa and in the naval war in the Mediterranean. It was widely believed by the Allied high command that the new Italian

A Lancaster which crashed on landing at Elsham Wolds due to damage
sustained over Germany.
(David W. Fell and RAF Elsham Wolds Association)

government, led by Marshal Badoglio, would want to make peace but feared to do so because of likely reprisals from Germany.

Harris was ordered to launch a series of heavy raids on industrial targets in Italy to put pressure on Badoglio. To ram the point home several aircraft on each raid dropped leaflets reading: 'Your government in Rome says the war continues. That is why our bombardment continues.' The bombing began in earnest on 7 August with a raid on Milan and another on Turin.

Over Milan a 44 Squadron bomber piloted by Herbert Barley was attacked by an Italian fighter that was faster and packed a tougher punch than those met before. It was probably a Macchi C205 Veltro. The Italian swooped and dived with deadly efficiency, then broke off the combat. The

Lancaster had lost two engines and was riddled with holes. Barley and his flight engineer did some quick calculations and realised that they stood no chance at all of returning to Waddington. Instead the navigator plotted a course for North Africa. Wrestling with the controls every inch of the way, Barley got his crippled aircraft across the Mediterranean and put it down safely on the sands of Tunisia.

After Italy did, indeed, surrender, Bomber Command returned its attentions to Germany. In September a raid was made on Hanover with 61 Squadron contributing several aircraft. One was flown by Pilot Officer Anthony Bird. As the aircraft began its bombing run it was caught by one of the new blue searchlights, and then coned by several others. Immediately three night-fighters zeroed in to the attack, opening fire with cannon and machine guns to devastating effect. One of the bomber's engines was set on fire and the aircraft seriously damaged.

The Lancaster suddenly lurched into a spiralling dive that Bird was quite unable to control. Flight engineer B. Kendrick came to the cockpit to help and together the two men wrestled the aircraft back into level flight. Wireless operator E. Kemish then took over from Kendrick while the latter went off to make running repairs to the aircraft. Now only a short distance from the target area, which Bird could see was illuminated by the firebombs and flares of other bombers, the crew held a quick discussion over the intercom and decided to push on. They bombed Hanover successfully, and only then turned for home. All three men, Bird, Kemish and Kendrick, were decorated for their actions.

In the summer of 1943 Harris decided it was time to return to raids on Berlin. Since the disastrous attack of November 1941, raids on the Reich capital had ceased for over a year. In January 1943 Harris sent a force to bomb the city under pressure from the Russians, but the results were disappointing and losses heavy at 8%. Harris used the short nights as a reason to call off any more raids on Berlin, but in November this excuse no longer held. Nor was Harris so set against the idea of target-Berlin. His bombers now had H2S to guide them so their raids could be relied upon to hit the target. They also had the so-called 'Fishpond', an on-board radar set that could detect approaching night-fighters, though it was not the most reliable set of electronics in operation.

On 23 September a raid on Berlin was made to test the effectiveness of H2S over the city and to probe German defences before the first major operation was undertaken. Among those flying was the crew of Flight

The crew of Flight Lieutenant D.W. Finlay DFC pose beside their Lancaster before the fateful raid to Berlin on 23 September 1944. (David W. Fell and RAF Elsham Wolds Association)

Lieutenant D.W. Finlay DFC of 103 Squadron. The navigator was Sergeant J.H. McFarlane. The crew was nearing the end of its tour of duty, having been together since April and having completed 23 attacks on the Ruhr, Dortmund, Hanover and Turin among other targets.

The raid of 23 September 1943 was the crew's first to Berlin. They were scheduled to be in the front of the first wave of the stream of bombers. This was as they wanted it for they firmly believed this was the safest position for a bomber to be in, getting away from the target before the night-fighters

After the war McFarlane (right) travelled to Germany to meet Siegfried Beugel (left), the Luftwaffe pilot who had shot him down.
(David W. Fell and RAF Elsham Wolds Association)

could gather. Unfortunately engine trouble delayed them and they arrived some ten minutes behind schedule.

McFarlane was completing his final calculations to take the Lancaster over the aiming point when a night-fighter dived on the bomber, spraying cannon shells into the port wing. The fuel tank immediately caught fire, illuminating the black crosses on the fighter as it swept past. The bomber was clearly doomed, so Finlay ordered the crew to bale out. Two men died, but the other five landed safely. Being so deep inside Germany they had no hope of escape and were duly arrested by the Germans.

They were taken to Frankfurt for interrogation at a Luftwaffe holding centre before being moved to a prisoner of war camp. There they met an American crew shot down a few days later than they had been. The night after their arrival, the drone of bomber engines filled the skies. One American peered out of the cell window and reported that he could see 'fireworks' falling from the sky. McFarlane pushed him aside and was startled to see familiar target marker flares coming down close by. The RAF men dived for cover, dragging the Americans with them just as the bombs came down on the markers. Fortunately no bombs fell on the holding centre.

Some years after the war McFarlane decided to find out more about their final mission. Through the German Night-Fighter Aircrew Association he made contact with former Feldwebel Siegfried Beugel who had been radar operator in the night-fighter that had shot him down. They met in 1976 and kept in touch for many years afterwards.

On this same raid a Lancaster of 101 Squadron flew out of Ludford Magna, only to be coned by searchlights over the German capital. The bomber was pounced on by a patrolling fighter, which set the inner port engine on fire. The pilot, Arthur Walker, put his aircraft into a dive to evade the attacker while the onboard extinguisher dealt with the flames. Meanwhile, a second fire had broken out inside the fuselage. The

The memorial to the men who served at Ludford Magna airfield.
(http://www.oldairfields.fotopic.net/)

flight engineer, Stan Meyer, went to work on the flames. He managed to beat out the fire, then fell unconscious from smoke inhalation. When he came round half an hour later, he insisted on getting back to his post to monitor the crucial readings from his instruments to allow Walker to get back to Ludford Magna. Both men were given the CGM.

Raids on other cities continued and in October a major force was sent against Kassel. Over the target a Lancaster flown by Kenneth Ames of 61 Squadron was attacked by a fighter. The German came tearing in from the rear, pouring cannonfire into the bomber's fuselage. Both tail gunner and upper gunner returned fire; their concentrated cone of bullets coming from six machine guns pummelled the enemy, tearing a wing off at its roots and sending the German aircraft plunging to its doom.

There was no respite, however, for even as the first fighter fell to earth, two more came into the fight. Ames threw the bomber around the sky in a series of violent moves that eventually shook off the attackers. Meanwhile, the upper turret had caught fire and the gunner's ammunition began going off in a series of staccato explosions. The navigator was wounded by the bullets flying around the aircraft, but the flight engineer managed to put out the flames and drag the wounded gunner from his turret to receive first aid.

Several systems were now out of action, but Ames managed to keep the bomber on an even keel. He made an emergency landing in East Anglia, ensuring his wounded colleagues got medical treatment quickly enough to save their lives.

.On 18 November Harris sent off the first major raid on Berlin by 400 heavy bombers. It was the forerunner of a series of raids that became known as the 'Battle of Berlin'. The campaign consumed much of the efforts of Bomber Command in the winter months.

It was on this operation that Flying Officer William Baker of 207 Squadron won a DFC after a most unfortunate accident. In the intense darkness of the night he began his bombing run, only for the aircraft to be suddenly jolted as if it had hit a brick wall. It had, in fact, hit the tail of another Lancaster, from 9 Squadron. The other Lancaster had its tail torn off and tail gunner killed, though the rest of the crew baled out successfully. Baker's aircraft lost its nose and the bomb-aimer fell to his death from the shattered nose. Gaining control of his aircraft, Baker decided to push on to Berlin regardless. Only when over the target did the crew find out that the bomb release gear did not work. They turned for home with the full bombload hanging ominously beneath the aircraft.

The wind that blew in through the open nose of the bomber was bitterly cold at 20,000 feet and the crew were soon numbed even though they wore thick flying gear. The first layer donned by aircrew was an all in one set of thermal underwear reaching from neck to ankle. Over this went the uniform battle dress, though some preferred a sweater to the collar and tie. Next came the so-called 'teddy-bear suit', a fleecy overall that zipped from crotch to neck. Finally came the flying suit itself, liberally adorned with zipped pockets. Feet were kept warm by two pairs of socks encased in knee-length sheepskin or fur-lined boots. The hands were covered first by a pair of thin silk gloves, then by woollen mittens and over all a pair of thick leather gauntlets. Around the neck was slung a whistle, with which to attract attention if they baled out and landed injured.

While his crew huddled in the fuselage, Baker was exposed to the full blast of the night air. By the time he landed back at Spilsby, Baker was so severely frostbitten that he was never again sent out on operational duties. He was awarded an immediate DFC.

The next raid took place on 23 November. Among those involved was Sergeant George Meadows, tail gunner in a Lancaster of 166 Squadron flying from Kirmington. As the aircraft lined up for its attack a night-fighter came in from beam, raking the bomber with cannonfire. Both the upper turret and the tail turret were damaged, with Meadows receiving a large piece of shrapnel in his back that caused an ugly, painful wound. The German came round again, this time Meadows kept up a running commentary on its movements, allowing the pilot to manoeuvre clear of the attack. In all the German attacked ten times, each time Meadows' calm courage enabled the bomber to survive. It was only after the fighter had disappeared in search of easier prey that Meadows revealed that he was injured and was given first aid. For his stoic courage despite being in great pain, Meadows was given a CGM.

As Christmas approached, the bomber crews began to encounter a disturbing new development among German night-fighters. A few German aircraft were equipped with a powerful searchlight. They used their radar to locate aircraft, then illuminated them for others to shoot down. Dubbed 'wild sow', these tactics led to heavy losses.

It was a 'wild sow' that caught the Lancaster flown by Flying Officer R.A. Randall of 460 Squadron over Berlin. The damaged bomber got as far as Denmark before it became clear it would never reach England. Randall

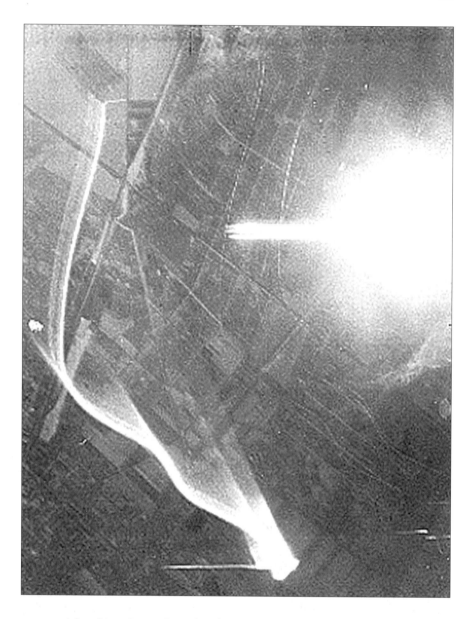

A bombing photo taken of Berlin in December 1943. By this date, all bombers took such photos as they dropped their bombs to help verify their claims to have hit the target.
(David W. Fell and RAF Elsham Wolds Association)

ordered the crew to bale out. Most landed on Danish soil, but Randall and his front gunner splashed down into the chill waters of the sea. They were promptly pulled out by the crew of a Swedish patrol boat, which took them back to Stockholm. Randall was back on operations within a month, but his second encounter with a 'wild sow' proved to be fatal and he was killed when his damaged Lancaster crashed on landing.

Also caught out by fighters was Flight Lieutenant Anthony Tomlin of the newly formed 619 Squadron who flew out of Strubby to attack Berlin on 16 December. The inner starboard engine was smashed to pieces by a hail of cannonfire and burst into flames. Flight engineer A. Brookes got the flames under control with the remote extinguisher but the engine was

The derelict control tower at Strubby. This was one of several new airfields that opened in the autumn of 1943.
(http://www.oldairfields.fotopic.net/)

*Now used for storage, these buildings were once the aircrew accommodation
blocks at Strubby airfield.
(http://www.oldairfields.fotopic.net/)*

useless and the wing badly damaged. He managed to restore the flow of
petrol to the outer engine, but it failed to reach full power. Effectively flying
on two engines, Tomlin got his bomber back to base, but then found the
undercarriage would not work.

As he began to gain height so that his crew could bale out, a third engine
packed up and Tomlin had no choice but to crash-land the stricken aircraft.
Lurching badly, the Lancaster came down in a shallow dive. Tomlin hauled
the nose up at the last moment and set the plane down in a field. The
bomber slithered across the grass at speed and tunnelled into a hedgerow.
Miraculously, nobody was injured and the entire crew walked away from
the wreckage.

On 30 January Canadian Pilot Officer Edgar Jones was aboard just one
of several Lancasters from 103 Squadron taking part in a raid on Berlin.
This was the crew's fourth journey to the Reich capital. As the aircraft
bored on through the night sky over Germany on its way to Berlin a hail of
bullets suddenly erupted through the floor of the fuselage close behind the
tail turret. The upper gunner saw the dark shape of an FW190 streak away

upwards as it passed by. There had been no warning of an approaching night-fighter nor had they been caught by searchlights. The damage suffered was extensive. The starboard tail fin and tail plane were riddled with holes and effectively useless. The tail turret was jammed solid and one of the bomb bay doors had been shot away.

As the upper gunner watched, the German fighter turned gracefully and came diving down to attack again. Jones threw the heavy bomber into a turning dive, but the German managed to hit the starboard wing and put one engine out of action. A third attack took place a few minutes later, but

Pilot Officer Edgar Jones (left) peers out through the hole in the side of his Lancaster caused by a German night-fighter over Berlin in January 1944. With him is Flying Office E Hooke. (David W. Fell and RAF Elsham Wolds Association)

Sgts. Mess, Elsham Wolds

CHRISTMAS DAY, 1943

Menu

Breakfast 08.00 to 09.00

Porridge or Corn Flakes with milk
Bacon and Egg
Bread Rolls and Butter
Toast and Marmalade
Tea or Coffee

Running Buffet 14.00

Dinner 18.30 to 19.30

SOUP
Julienne
Tomato

FISH
Fried Plaice and French Potatoes

POULTRY
Roast Goose
Roast Turkey
Stuffing

JOINT
Roast Pork, Sage and Onion Stuffing
Apple Sauce - Savoury Yorkshire
Roast and Creamed Potatoes
Brussels Sprouts
Dinner Cobs

SWEET
Christmas Pudding and Rum Sauce
Coffee   Cheese and Biscuits
Mince Pies   Apple Creams   Jam Tarts
Sausage Rolls
Apples   Oranges   Beer   Cigarettes

CHEF CUISINE - SGT. WOOLHOUSE

The Christmas Day menu card from Elsham Wolds. Despite wartime shortages and the hardships of active service, an effort was made to celebrate the festive season as well as possible. (David W. Fell and RAF Elsham Wolds Association)

A 5 Group Christmas party held in the sergeants' mess.
(David W. Fell and RAF Elsham Wolds Association)

this time the German missed the bomber and dived away to be seen no more.

Realising that the bomber would be unable to reach Berlin and return, Jones coolly flew his aircraft towards the known location of some heavy flak batteries and bombed them instead. He then turned for home, nursing the aircraft through the skies across the North Sea to return to base. He was awarded a DFC for his actions and on 24 February he and his crew were back over Germany, this time attacking Schweinfurt. Jones and his crew continued to bomb Germany until they had completed 27 raids, when they were taken off operational duties and sent to training stations. All of them survived the war.

Towards the end of the Battle of Berlin, Wing Commander Robert Bowes of 44 Squadron won a DFC and then a bar within a few weeks of each other. His first medal came when he continued with a bombing run, dropping his bombs from the pilot's seat after the bombsight was shattered and his bomb-aimer wounded by a flak shell. His second medal came when his bomber was again damaged during its bombing run. This time it was an engine that was blasted by flak shell, the wing around it being holed in more than two dozen places by shrapnel. Again, Bowes completed the run to drop his bombs accurately before turning for home. This time the aircraft proved to be mortally damaged. Bowes managed to nurse it over the North Sea to reach an emergency landing strip in East Anglia, but it was so badly damaged that it never flew again.

Although it was for these two raids that Bowes won his medals, he was widely respected throughout 5 Group for the care that he lavished on the new crews joining 44 Squadron, first at Waddington then at Dunholme Lodge. Whenever possible he kept the new crews on shorter missions at first so that they could gain experience before flying to distant or heavily defended targets. His leadership and skills at training crews were legendary.

Another pilot to win a DFC and bar was Henry Dixie Churchill, flying from Elsham Wolds. He won his first medal during an attack on Brunswick in January when an engine was set on fire by a flak shell. The flight engineer put out the fire with the remote extinguisher while Churchill pressed home the attack regardless.

More dramatic was the winning of a bar to the medal during an attack on Karlsruhe a few weeks later. This time two flak shells hit the aircraft almost simultaneously. The port wing was damaged by the blast of the first, and the starboard wing by the second. The fuel tank in the starboard wing was punctured and a stream of burning petrol cascaded out. This fountain of flame hit the fuselage just in front of the rear turret. The stream of burning fuel was short lived, but it had set fire to the fuselage.

Realising the danger to the rear gunner, flight engineer G. Meer grabbed the portable extinguishers and went to work on the blazing section of fuselage. Suddenly the oxygen supply failed, and soon Meer was getting lightheaded as he battled the flames. Churchill dived to lower altitude so that he and his men could breathe, and in doing so helped Meer put out the fire. At low level and in constant danger of the airframe breaking up, the aircraft raced over the North Sea to belly land in East Anglia. The crew survived, though several were injured.

By February 1944 the German defences were at their most effective. A chain of radar stations was positioned along the coasts of Europe from northern France to Denmark. These stations picked up the bomber formations as they left Britain. Night-fighter bases lay among the radar to launch attacks on the bombers as they crossed the coast. Running down the western frontier of Germany itself was another belt of radar to track the bombers as they crossed the continent. Once the likely target was identified, large numbers of night-fighters were sent up to intercept the bombers. A belt of searchlights and flak guns guarded the routes to the Ruhr, while a second guarded Berlin. In addition all important factories and towns had their own local batteries and fighter bases that operated to protect their immediate area. Germany was a very dangerous place to be at night.

It was in an attempt to find a way round these increasingly formidable defences, that members of 617 Squadron undertook their most dramatic raid since they demolished the dams. Harris had issued an edict that 617 was to be reserved as an 'old lags' squadron. This was the term he used for veterans who offered to fly on beyond their official tours of duty. Highly experienced and skilled, the 'old lags' were ideal for undertaking difficult missions. They were also skilled enough to try out, and even devise, new tactics.

One of the tactics that 617 developed was that of 'low marking'. They knew that Pathfinders were managing to mark targets with some accuracy, but all too often the original marker flares were wide of the actual target. In area-bombing raids this did not matter too much as the following bombers plastered the area around the markers, but the RAF was being asked to undertake an increasing number of precision raids at this time.

'Mickey' Martin came up with the answer. He was practising precision bombing by making runs at a patch of floating seaweed in the Wash when he realised that he could see it much better when diving on it than when approaching at low level in a flat trajectory. He discussed the idea with squadron commander Leonard Cheshire, who at once took off and found the same thing. He could bomb more accurately when diving than when approaching on the level. The two men reasoned that marking would also be more accurate.

They tried it unofficially on 21 January when attacking V1 launch sites in northern France. While the squadron circled at 12,000 feet, Munro dropped flares to illuminate the ground. Martin flew his aircraft down towards the target, pulling out of the dive at just 400 feet and dropping the marker flares. The rest of the squadron then bombed the markers. Reconnaissance the next day showed the unusual precision of this raid.

Cheshire then went to see Air Vice Marshal Cochrane, commanding officer of 5 Group, to ask for permission to repeat the tactic in a major raid. Cochrane at first refused because of the high casualties suffered by bombers at low level and the poor accuracy they attained. Cheshire, arguing that marking when diving was safer and more accurate than approaching at low level, persisted just long enough for Cochrane to remember a target that he had been banned from attacking by none other than Winston Churchill himself.

The Gnome-Rhone aircraft engine factory at Limoges had been turning out engines for the Germans ever since France surrendered. The destruction of the factory would be a serious blow to the Luftwaffe, but Churchill had vetoed an attack on two grounds. First, the factory was in the middle of a French town and inaccurate area bombing would kill many French civilians. Second, the Germans were working the factory on round the clock shifts so that it was never empty of French workers. Even accurate bombing would, therefore, inflict unacceptable casualties on civilians of an allied country.

Cochrane, however, thought that the new idea from 617 might offer a way to attack the Gnome-Rhone factory. The method of dive marking offered high precision, while the noise of a mighty four-engined Lancaster diving over the factory at just 400 feet would give the 300 French women working in the factory ample warning of the coming raid. Churchill was still unconvinced, so Cheshire offered to make three dives on the factory before bombing began. The raid was given the go ahead.

To make the raid doubly important the Lancasters were equipped with brand new 12,000 pound bombs. These were expected to inflict massive blast damage. This raid would test them.

Twelve Lancasters of 617 Squadron took off on the 8 February 1944 and arrived over Limoges in bright moonlight. The town had never been attacked and the blackout was bad. There were enough lights showing for Cheshire to identify the factory with ease. His navigator, Pat Kelly, peered down from the cockpit and declared that he could see a little bistro with a pretty waitress just waiting for them. Cheshire told him to shut up and hit the factory.

Down went Cheshire's Lancaster, roaring over the factory roof at barely 300 feet with all engines on full throttle. He climbed away, then turned and dived again. This time Kelly saw hundreds of figures streaming from the buildings and running into the town. On the third pass, Cheshire reached just 50 feet, then let go of his incendiaries. Circling just above him, Martin saw the fire bombs fall, then he too dived down to plant red marker flares in the centre of the factory complex. It was one minute past midnight.

At one minute intervals the remaining bombers flew over the factory, dropping their massive bombs with absolute precision. Cheshire circled for a while, but could see nothing but smoke.

Next morning a reconnaissance photograph revealed that the factory had ceased to exist. Not even the walls were still standing. And the bomb craters of the mighty 12,000 pounders overlapped neatly. Not a single house had been hit, though several were missing roof tiles and few had intact windows. A few weeks later a letter reached the RAF in London through a neutral country. It was signed by the nightshift girls of Gnome-Rhone and thanked the pilot of the low-flying aircraft for warning them of the raid. Enticingly it added that one or two of the women would like to thank the pilot very personally if he called after the war was over.

It took time to train the crews and convince officialdom, but the dive-marking tactic would later become standard throughout Bomber Command. And it would be even more effective when an aircraft more nimble than the lumbering Lancaster was used. But that lay in the future.

On 25 February 103 Squadron was sent to bomb Augsburg. One of the Lancasters was flown by William Eddy, who had been living in Argentina when the war broke out, but left his wife and children to volunteer for the RAF. This was to be his 16th operation over Germany, and by far the most eventful.

The flight out was more or less routine, the Lancaster climbing to 23,000 feet before bombing the target rather later than most of the other aircraft. Searchlights and flak were evaded as Eddy steered away from Augsburg, but moments later a stray shell exploded just below the Lancaster's now empty bomb bay. The resulting fire blazed through the hydraulic system, causing the bomb bay doors to flap open and filling the fuselage with chocking smoke. The flight engineer passed out, though he was otherwise uninjured, while the crew tackled the fire. By the time all the fire extinguishers had been used up the fire was still blazing fiercely, so Eddy ordered his crew to gather to bale out, while he dived the aircraft down to 10,000 feet.

As the aircraft dived, the rushing wind blew out the fire, so he climbed to 15,000 feet and sent the crew back to their stations. Very quickly, however, it was realised that the aircraft was losing fuel at a rapid rate, probably through a hole in a main fuel line. The navigator worked out the most direct route to occupied France and Eddy once again gathered the crew for baling out. Only at this point did Eddy realise that the fire had burned

The staff of the airmen's mess pose outside the mess hut at Elsham Wolds. The ancillary staff were vital to keeping the squadron flying.

through the base of his seat and destroyed his parachute. Nevertheless, he sent the crew baling out to parachute to safety while he remained at the controls.

The official report, written later, takes up the story: 'After the crew had gone the port outer engine gave out, followed by the other three in rapid succession. Ft/Lt Eddy feathered the propellers and glided downwards maintaining a speed of about 150 mph. From 4,000 ft he could see the ground covered with snow against which the woods stood out clearly as dark patches. The Navigator had warned him that he was over the wooded Ardennes country with hills running up to 600 ft. He switched on the landing lights for a few seconds but the glare on the snow was blinding so he switched off again. At about 600 ft he levelled out, finding himself above a small town. He passed close over the roof tops and a small wood beyond and down into an open patch with 3 or 4 ft of snow. The Lancaster hit the ground gently once, bounced forward and touched down again rather more violently. As his harness straps had been burnt away, Ft/Lt Eddy was thrown forward against the windscreen, hitting his head. He was unconscious for a short while and when he came to the Lancaster had come to rest against a fence.'

Having set fire to the wrecked Lancaster, Eddy set off through the snow. He could speak a few words of French and was, naturally, fluent in Spanish though with a heavy Argentinian accent. He made contact with a farmer, who gave him directions to a village some miles away where the Resistance was hiding an American airman shot down a few weeks earlier. The two men were passed from one Resistance group to the next across France over the following weeks and by April were trekking over the Pyrenees into Spain. There Eddy's Spanish allowed them to evade internment and to reach the British Embassy in Madrid.

Eddy returned to Elsham Wolds in early May 1944 together with a case of Spanish wine and another of sherry. He was, there is no need to say, very popular. He was awarded a DSO for his actions and completed his tour. Eddy later served in Mosquitoes with the Pathfinders, completing another 60 missions to win a DFC and bar. He survived the war to return to Argentina and his family.

Eddy's Spanish wine was not the only factor in boosting the morale of the men serving in Lincolnshire at this time. Quite unknown to each other, two of Britain's future showbiz stars were in Bomber Command. At North Coates, a non-operational support station, a young engine fitter from London decided to relieve the boredom by putting on an amateur revue

A vital task carried out by the women of the WAAF was to inspect and fold parachutes prior to each mission. Many aircrew owed their lives to the skill of these ladies. This parachute folding team is from Elsham Wolds.
(David W. Fell and RAF Elsham Wolds Association)

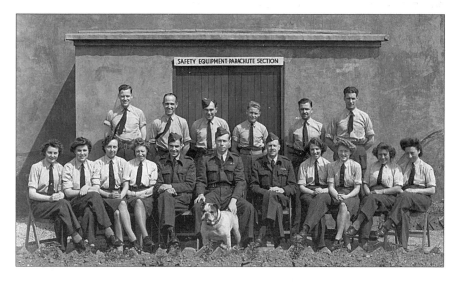

Sport was often used to relieve the long periods of monotony experienced by men living on remote airfields miles away from home and family. This football team was put together at Elsham Wolds. (David W. Fell and RAF Elsham Wolds Association)

show called *Chocks Away*. Based on life with 143, 236 and 254 Squadrons, which flew from North Coates, the show took some liberties with local personalities and those in command. The show proved enormously popular and encouraged the young man to take to the stage professionally after the war. His name was Max Bygraves.

Very different was the wartime career of a future member of the Goons comedy team. Michael Bentine was serving with 12 Squadron at Wickenby. Bentine did not think his role as Intelligence Officer was compatible with stage comedy, so he kept off the boards during the war. Later he would pay tribute time and again to his years in the RAF and the many men he briefed for their missions.

In March 1944 the entire strategy of Bomber Command was fundamentally changed. Attacks on Berlin and other German cities were to continue, though in much reduced strength. Instead the great bombers were to be employed preparing the way for the landings in Normandy to take place on what became known as D-Day. Bomber Command was entering a new era.

Junkers Ju88C

Type:	Night-fighter
Engines:	2 x 1,400 hp Junkers Jumo 211JB
Wingspan:	65 ft 10 in
Length:	47 ft 1 in
Height:	16 ft 7 in
Weight:	Empty 18,871 lb
	Loaded 27,226 lb
Armament:	3 x 20 mm cannon and 3 x 7.92 mm machine guns in nose, plus 1 x 13 mm machine gun in rear cockpit, plus 2 x 20 mm cannon firing upwards
Max speed:	311 mph
Ceiling:	32,000 ft
Range:	1,230 miles
Production:	3,200

The Junkers Ju88 was designed as a high-speed medium bomber in 1936 but in 1939 the addition of more powerful engines made a fighter-bomber version possible. With the increasing impact of RAF Bomber Command's campaign against Germany, a further modification led to the development of the Ju88C night-fighter variant. The bomb bay was removed and its place taken up by airborne radar, which enabled the third crew member to direct the pilot to the bombers. In early 1944 production of the Ju88C was halted in favour of the new Ju88G, which had a completely redesigned fuselage housing more sophisticated radar and electronic countermeasures as well as improved weaponry. This aircraft accounted for more RAF bombers than all other models of Luftwaffe fighters combined.

Chapter 8

Reaping the Whirlwind

In March 1944 Harris was ordered to take the full strength of Bomber Command off Germany and instead direct it to France. The proposed D-Day landings that would take the Allied armies into Europe by way of Normandy were only a few weeks away. The high command deemed it necessary to use the heavy bombers to prepare the way.

The move was not without controversy. The targets Harris was asked to hit were primarily rail junctions, road bridges and road junctions with garrison camps and ammunition dumps as secondary objectives. Most of these were in or near French towns, meaning that stray bombs would kill French civilians. Harris argued that while specialist squadrons, such as 617 Dambusters, could hit such targets, the majority of his force were not trained in precision bombing and would most likely inflict massive collateral damage and, perhaps, miss what they were aiming at as well. Harris preferred to send his heavy bombers against only those targets that lay outside French towns, and keep the bulk of his force pounding at German industry. He argued that destroying German tank factories was just as effective as halting their progress to Normandy by blowing up bridges.

Churchill, Portal and others recognised that Harris had a point. Unfortunately they did not have enough low-level medium bombers flown by crews with precision-bombing training to do the job instead.

Harris was overruled.

In the following weeks Harris sent his bombers again and again to France. They totally destroyed 60% of the targets they were given, and put another 30% out of action for varying lengths of time. It was a fantastic achievement, but Harris had been proved sadly right in one respect. His main force was not accurate enough to avoid heavy civilian casualties. Bombing the rail depot at Lille caused 456 French deaths and the attack on a target at Ghent killed 482 Belgians. Elsewhere the totals were lower, but no less damaging to morale among both Harris's crews and the civilians awaiting liberation from German rule.

One such raid was the attack on 3 May on a panzer depot near the village of Mailly-le-Camp. The raid proved to be a disaster for the RAF after signalling failures meant the message from the master bomber to begin the attack were not picked up by the main force. As a result the bombers were left circling over France longer than they should have been, allowing night-fighters to concentrate and shoot down 42 bombers. Among those brought down was a Lancaster of 12 Squadron flying out of Wickenby. The navigator was a 31-year-old Londoner named Maurice Garlick, who landed with burned legs in a field near Romilly.

As Garlick was able only to crawl, it took him two days to reach the cover of a small wood about two miles from where he landed and three days more to reach a farmhouse he could see beyond the trees. The farmer and his daughter dressed his wounds and gave him food and drink but refused to let him stay for fear of German reprisals. By 14 May he had run out of food so he knocked at another farm, near Bucy. Garlick had by luck arrived at the house of Charles Decreon, the head of the local Resistance group.

Garlick was given medical aid and a bed to rest in. On 29 May he was joined by his crewmate Paddy O'Hara and a few days later by John Crighton, also from the downed crew. One day in July the Gestapo arrived to carry out a random search of the farm. The three fugitives fled to nearby woods, escaping just minutes before their hiding place was searched. On 10 August they left Decreon's house to join an active Resistance group in the densely wooded Forest d'Othe. Arms were dropped to the group by the RAF and soon the three downed airmen were joining the band of Frenchmen in attacking German outposts and patrols.

On 2 September an American armoured column arrived in the forest to drive the Germans from the area. The three RAF men were quickly sent

The crew of Squadron Leader H. Swanston (above) included the cheerful chemistry teacher Ron Boyd (below right). Their aircraft was shot down over Mailly-le-Camp and all were killed.
(David W. Fell and RAF Elsham Wolds Association)

off back to newly-liberated Paris and thence to Britain. Back at Wickenby they met their pilot, Peter Maxwell, who had walked to Spain with the aid of the Resistance. All four men survived the war.

The crew of another Lancaster shot down that same night was less fortunate. The plane was piloted by Squadron Leader H. Swanston and contained a mixed crew of Britons, Canadians and Australians, including Ron Boyd, a chemistry teacher from Australia who had volunteered for service in the RAF in 1940. This Lancaster was attacked by a night-fighter, burst instantly into flames and crashed near Villers-le-Chateau. The remains of the crew were recovered from the wreck and buried in the village churchyard.

Even those who survived this dreadful night had ordeals to face. Sergeant Richard Robert Reed of 576 Squadron flew from Elsham Wolds with a crew that had accompanied him on 14 missions already.

The bomber was attacked as it circled by a Ju88 night-fighter. As the cannon shells tore into the bomber, Reed felt it lurch out of control into a diving turn. As Reed wrestled with the control column, the flight engineer, Sergeant Arthur Taylor, moved forward to lend a hand. The two men managed to drag the column back to get the bomber flying level, but the effort was such that the Canadian bomb-aimer, Michael Saruk, had to be summoned to work the rudder pedals with his hands. Having got the aircraft under control, Reed assessed the damage. The compass was

Air and ground crew of a 576 Squadron Lancaster pose beside their aircraft at Elsham Wolds airfield.
(David W. Fell and RAF Elsham Wolds Association)

'Nose Art' is often thought of as an American invention, but the RAF could also decorate their aircraft with saucy pictures of attractive young ladies dealing out death to the enemy, as shown by this Lancaster of 576 Squadron piloted by R.J. Edie. (David W. Fell and RAF Elsham Wolds Association)

broken, the wireless set out of action, the oxygen supply system destroyed and extensive holes riddled the elevators and rudders.

Further back in the fuselage a vast hole had been torn in the floor and a fire was blazing. The upper gunner promptly baled out, but wireless operator George Hallows went to work on the fire.

At this point the long awaited markers were dropped on the target. Despite the damage to the bomber, Reed turned it towards the glowing lights and dropped his bombs with accuracy. He then turned back to the task of getting home. First, however, the fire in the fuselage attracted a second Ju88 and further damage was sustained by the Lancaster. Taylor scrambled back to investigate and joined Hallows in putting out the fire. He then edged along the fuselage to find the rear gunner dead and his

A ground crew of 576 Squadron stop for a cup of tea, brewed up by the hard-working ladies of the NAAFI. Regular brew-ups were vital to maintaining morale on airfields.
(David W. Fell and RAF Elsham Wolds Association)

*A Flight of 576 Squadron poses in front of a Lancaster.
(David W. Fell and RAF Elsham Wolds Association)*

turret smashed almost beyond recognition.

As they flew north in the crippled bomber, Hallows got the radio working and signalled ahead to alert the station to the condition of the aircraft. On touching down the starboard undercarriage leg of the Lancaster collapsed and the bomber swung off the runway, skidding sideways and coming to a standstill with smoke pouring from one of its engines. The five surviving crew members scrambled from the wreckage. Each of them was given a medal for the night's work, but sadly none lived long enough to collect their awards. On 22 May their new aircraft was shot down over Dortmund and they were all killed.

Later in May disaster almost struck the entire D-Day invasion plan. The base at Elsham Wolds received a new commander in the shape of Air Commodore Ronald Ivelaw-Chapman. Having spent the previous year working as a staff officer at Air Ministry, he was all too aware that the realities of air combat had moved on since his last mission, and even more so since he had won a DFC in a fighter over France in 1918. His first move was, therefore, to fly on board a Lancaster of 576 Squadron on a short raid into Normandy. Unfortunately the aircraft was shot down, though the men got out safely.

When the news was sent from Elsham Wolds to the Air Ministry there was sudden panic. Ivelaw-Chapman had been responsible for planning much of the air offensive that was taking place and he knew both the date and place set for D-Day. Fortunately Ivelaw-Chapman had thought to don the uniform of a pilot for the raid. His interrogation was routine and the Germans never realised just who they had.

Typical of the targets in France that Harris preferred was the mighty gun battery at Cap Griz Nez outside Calais. It was easy to find and well away from any vulnerable civilians. Just before D-Day, the task of destroying it was given to 300 Squadron based at Faldingworth. This Polish squadron sent up 15 Lancasters, which swept in toward the French coast in broad daylight to ensure accurate bombing. The first aircraft in was that flown by Pilot Officer Stepien. Passing right over the heavy guns, the bomb-aimer had a clear sight of his target but when he pressed the bomb release button, nothing happened. Three times Stepien braved the heavy flak, but each time the bombs stubbornly refused to fall. Stepien then had to fly his damaged Lancaster back to base with a full bombload and land as gingerly as possible. The aircraft safely came to a halt, when it was discovered that a wiring fault had caused the problem.

Flight engineer John Edward Jennings (right) was flying in the Lancaster piloted by the Canadian Flying Officer Wilfred Howard Way (left) when both were shot down and killed on D-Day. (David W. Fell and RAF Elsham Wolds Association)

On D-Day itself, the Lincolnshire squadrons were exceptionally busy. From Elsham Wolds, 103 Squadron was sent off to attack railway bridges at Vire in northern France. Among the squadron was the crew of the Canadian Flying Officer Wilfred Howard Way RCAF in the Lancaster 'E'. The crew had been together since training in February and had completed almost a full tour. Their rear gunner had left after the previous mission, having completed his tour early by flying with other crews on four missions.

Flying with Way was flight engineer John Edward Jennings, a Yorkshireman, while the rest of the crew was made up of Canadians and Australians. In all 107 Lancasters from 1 Group were to attack the key bridges that were carrying German reinforcements to Normandy to oppose the D-Day landings. The flight out was unremarkable, but over the French coast dense cloud set in that totally obscured the target. The Pathfinders led the bomber stream down to 3,000 feet to be below the cloud. The low altitude made the bombers more vulnerable to flak but being low was felt necessary to ensure accurate bombing and so avoid French civilian casualties.

About five minutes from the target Way's Lancaster was attacked by a night-fighter. Both wings caught fire, but Way pushed on while the air gunners returned fire and sent the German down in flames. Way managed to drop his bombs with great accuracy, then turned away to port, still trailing flames from both wings. He seems to have attempted a crash-landing in a field at Maisonseule, about 2 miles north-east of Vire. Witnesses say the Lancaster hit the ground at a very shallow angle, which broke off the tail.

The site at Maisonseule, France where Way's Lancaster crashed in flames.
(David W. Fell and RAF Elsham Wolds Association)

The main section of the aircraft continued at some speed to slide along the ground, shedding burning wreckage and coming to rest yards from a farmhouse. Tragically there were no survivors from the crew. It is impossible to say with certainty what happened in the last few minutes of the flight but it seems reasonable to suggest that this was a valiant attempt by the pilot to crash-land his crippled aircraft and save his gallant crew who had stuck together to the end.

Throughout this period, Harris did continue to attack targets in Germany. He argued that if raids on the Reich stopped completely, the Germans would be able to move their fighters and flak guns to France. These raids were, however, smaller and less frequent than those in the previous months, and those that were to come.

A key target was the industrial town of Schweinfurt in southern Germany. This was the centre for German ball bearing production, and without ball bearings most modern machinery cannot function. The American 8th Air Force had already tried to bomb the factories by daylight, but their losses had been so horrific that they suspended long-range raids into Germany. The job was given to the RAF flying at night. Among the squadrons that took off for this heavily defended town on 26 April was 106 operating out of Metherington.

Flying Officer Fred Mifflin was flying O Orange, with Norman Jackson as his flight engineer. It was the 30th and final mission of the crew's tour of duty. The raid went to plan, with Mifflin's Lancaster dropping bombs accurately on the marker flares. As the aircraft turned for home, however, it was attacked from behind by a night-fighter. Cannon shells riddled the fuselage and punctured the starboard wing, setting the inner engine on fire.

Jackson at once set off the engine's extinguisher, but this only damped down the blaze instead of putting it out. Mifflin was preparing to order his crew to bale out before the fire reached the wing fuel tank and blew the aircraft apart when Jackson's voice came on the intercom.

'I think I can deal with it, Fred,' he said.

'How?' asked Mifflin.

'I'll get out there with an extinguisher. That should fix it.'

Not certain he had heard Jackson correctly, Mifflin agreed and struggled to keep the stricken bomber flying level.

Jackson opened the hatch that gave access to the upper surface of the wing. Before climbing out he pulled the ripcord of his parachute and handed the silk canopy to bomb-aimer Maurice Toft and navigator Fred Higgins. He told them to pay out the parachute slowly as he climbed over the wing, and if he fell to let go so that he stood a chance of floating to earth. The plan seemed crazy, but it was the only chance of saving the aircraft.

Tucking an extinguisher into his jacket, Jackson climbed out of the aircraft into the howling slipstream of bitterly cold air whipping past the fuselage. Kicking holes in the fabric of the fuselage to give himself footholds, Jackson scrambled down onto the wing. He grabbed the air intakes on the leading edge with his hands and inched out toward the burning engine. He pushed the extinguisher into the engine and set it off. The spurting foam quickly got the flames under control.

At that instant the Lancaster suddenly banked to port as a stream of cannon shells poured into it and slashed into Jackson's legs. He lost his grip on the wing and fell backwards into the night sky. His fall was momentarily stopped as his parachute cords snapped taut. Jackson was now dangling behind the bomber, catching a momentary glimpse of the startled face of rear gunner Sergeant Hugh Johnson peering at him from the turret. Then Toft and Higgins paid out the parachute and Jackson was floating gently to earth. Above him the doomed Lancaster caught fire and dived to earth. Toft and Higgins got out in time, as did two others, but Johnson and Mifflin both died.

Jackson hit the ground hard, spraining both ankles to add to his cannon wounds in both legs and burned hands. He managed to crawl to a house, to be greeted with contempt by the German within and denied medical care of any kind until a military patrol turned up some hours later. Transferred to a prisoner of war camp, Jackson spent 10 months in hospital. When he emerged it was to learn he had been given the Victoria Cross for his exploits.

On the night of the 21/22 May 1944 the men of Lincolnshire took off to attack Duisberg in the Ruhr. Among the crews was that led by Canadian Pilot Officer T.I. Jones of 103 Squadron. This aircraft was hit by flak and then finished off by a night-fighter flown by Hauptmann Martin Drewes of III/NJG 1. Drewes was a highly decorated night-fighter pilot and shot down 49 bombers, all but 2 by night. He survived the war.

The Lancaster crashed near Zwolle in Holland, four of the crew having baled out successfully. Pilot Officer Jones, Sergeant Pickles and Sergeant W.E. Jones failed to get out in time and were killed. Two more – Sergeant Sharp and Sergeant Francis – escaped capture and managed to make

An advert placed in a national magazine by Short Brothers in July 1944. Although it optimistically states the Stirling is the company's contribution to the night bomber offensive, the Stirling had by this date been transferred to second line duties such as transport, glider tug or the bombing of targets in France. Of course, at the time strict wartime censorship would have made the claim hard to disprove.

contact with the Dutch Resistance who kept them safe until they could reach Allied ground forces. The two remaining crew members, Warrant Officer Davis and Warrant Officer Moran, were captured by the Germans after hiding out with the help of Dutch farmers for some weeks. Warrant Officer Davis had been wounded in the aerial combat, and was subjected to the full horrors of a Gestapo interrogation. His treatment was so severe that he was repatriated in February 1945. He returned to Australia in a hospital ship and was only finally fit to be released from hospital in 1948. In 1977 he was able to return to Holland with his wife and visited some places he had been in during the war and contacted the Dutch people who had helped him.

Once the Allied armies were ashore, Bomber Command was asked to continue with their attacks on transport links for several weeks. Most of these raids were flown at night and, since the targets were relatively close to England, electronic aids meant that accuracy was high.

One raid that went wrong was that on Revigny on 12 July. The target was a railway junction and marshalling yards that were crucial to the German's supply system, but French houses and flats lay close by so pinpoint accuracy was essential. A master bomber was sent to direct the raid, assisted by Pathfinders with marker flares. Bad weather forced the raid to be postponed three times, and it was eventually decided to combine the Revigny raid, alloted to 1 Group, with a 5 Group attack on a similar target at Culmont 50 miles to the south. At first all went well, but low cloud closed in as the formations approached their targets. As at Mailly, the Lancasters were forced to circle while the targets were identified by the master bomber. Again, night-fighters closed in and casualties mounted. This time the master bomber called off the raid, sending the Lancasters home before things got too serious.

But for some it was already too late. The first that rear gunner Sergeant P.H. Keeler knew of the trouble was when he felt his Lancaster lurch as if hit by a giant fist. Moments later he realised that the intercom was out of action and that one wing was on fire. Unable to contact the rest of the crew, Keeler watched as the fire grew, then decided to bale out. He saw one other parachute open, but then lost contact as the wind blew him eastward. He was picked up by the Resistance and smuggled back to England, where he wrote a letter to the family of his pilot, Claude Hart.

'I am sorry I cannot give you any real news of Claude, as unfortunately in the first part of the attack the intercom was put out of action and so I know

Claude Hart, who was shot down in July 1944 but whose fate remained a mystery for over a year.

nothing about the five boys in the front of the plane. The only person I saw was Glenny who jumped out after me, but I know Glenny was told to jump by one of the five in the front of the aircraft. When I jumped out the wing and 2 engines were on fire. As my parachute opened it knocked me out so I never saw where the plane crashed, but I worked out where it should have crashed and the Underground French told me that there were about eleven lads down safely in the district.'

Unfortunately, none of the other men in Keeler's aircraft had survived. Unknown to him the men reported by the 'Underground French' were from other bombers shot down that night. It was not until after the war that the truth was discovered.

Also brought down that night was the Lancaster flown by Raymond Linklater, out of Elsham Wolds. The bomber broke up in the air, crashing to the ground in two sections. The front part, still carrying its bombs, was blown to pieces as it landed; the rear section landed completely intact. The tail gunner inside was, however, dead – though there was not a single mark on his body. The remains of the men were gathered up by the local French farmers and buried at Loches-sur-Ource. The burial service was a grand affair, attended the local mayor and a large crowd of civilians keen to show their support for the Allies and animosity to the Germans.

More worrying for Harris and his crews than missions to attack targets behind German lines, was the request to co-operate closely with the ground forces. Such joint operations called for even greater precision. The series reached a climax on 18 July when 863 heavy bombers pounded German positions during a ground attack codenamed 'Goodwood'. The attack failed to achieve its objectives due to clever German counterattacks. Harris was unimpressed, but as ever followed orders and continued the missions.

One such operation saw five Lancasters of 101 Squadron take off from Ludford Magna to attack a panzer camp sighted by reconnaissance near Paris. The formation was attacked by German fighters as it approached the target. One bomber was literally torn in half by a blast of cannonfire from a Messerschmitt 110. The front half, containing the bombs, exploded killing all inside, but the rear part of the fuselage fell clear.

In the tail turret, Sergeant Jack Worsford recovered from the shock of the initial blow to find that his turret was jammed in such a position that the door would not open. As the tail section fell, it spun causing Worsford to become dizzy and disorientated as he prepared himself for what seemed to be inevitable death. Suddenly the downward spiral came to a halt as

In July 1944 the Lancaster flown by Raymond Linklater (above left) was brought down over France. Linklater and most of the crew died when the main part of the aircraft (above right) struck the ground and exploded, but the tail gunner William McCollum (below left) died in the tail section (below right) which hit the ground almost a mile away. (David W. Fell and RAF Elsham Wolds Association)

Flying Officer A.V. J. 'Selmo' Vernieuwe and his crew pose beside their Lancaster after their eventful first mission over Germany. (David W. Fell and RAF Elsham Wolds Association)

the section of aircraft hit high-tension power cables. These flung the tail turret back into the air, spinning into the branches of a tree, which cushioned the impact.

Worsford hung for some minutes in his harness, before finally coming to terms with his remarkable escape. He smashed his way out of his turret and climbed down from the tree to find himself arrested by a passing German patrol.

Harris was furious when, on 14 August, another major attack in support of ground troops went badly wrong. The RAF were told to use yellow marker flares, but the Canadian ground troops were ordered to light yellow flares to mark their front line. Inevitably some bombers targeted the Canadians, killing 80 soldiers. The close support missions were called off.

By the end of August 1944 the only raids Harris and Bomber Command were undertaking in France were against isolated targets such as the

V1 launch pads or transport links outside towns. The main effort was concentrated once again on Germany. It was now that Harris's prediction made four long years earlier was to come true. He had said that the Germans bombing London were sowing the wind. Now Germany was about to reap the whirlwind. The RAF was operating bombers in larger numbers and carrying heavier bombs than any the Luftwaffe had sent over Britain. Slowly and methodically the bombers were to reduce the industrial cities of the Reich to rubble.

It was on one such raid that the Lancaster flown by Flying Officer Steve Nunns of 630 Squadron from East Kirby was hit by flak. The port inner engine burst into flames, the fire spreading rapidly to the fuel tank in the wing. Nunns held the stricken aircraft steady while his crew baled out,

Flying Officer Vernieuwe sits in the cockpit of his beloved Lancaster M Mother. (David W. Fell and RAF Elsham Wolds Association)

then engaged the autopilot and clambered toward the escape hatch in the nose. As he paused before jumping, Nunns glanced toward the port wing and was amazed to see that the fire had gone out.

Hurriedly scrambling back to his seat, Nunns disengaged the autopilot and took control. He then turned for home and flew back without incident. Needless to say the ground crew at East Kirby were amazed when Nunns alone climbed out of the heavy bomber on his return. The crew all landed safely close to the front line and managed to get back to England.

Equally fortunate was Flying Officer A.V.J. 'Selmo' Vernieuwe – a Belgian pilot serving with the Royal Air Force who flew his first mission over Germany with 103 Squadron from Elsham Wolds. The raid of 412 bombers was to the Opel motor factory at Russelheim on 25 August 1944. Vernieuwe's novice crew, in Lancaster M Mother, took off at 8.22 pm and found good weather all the way to the target. For a new crew the heavy flak and weaving searchlights must have been unnerving as they made their bombing run, but were as nothing to what came next.

The Focke Wulf 190 entered service in 1942 and quickly proved to be Germany's most effective fighter.

A rare daylight shot taken from a Lancaster raiding Flushing on 17 September 1944. By this time daylight raids on coastal targets were beginning to be made as Allied fighters could provide adequate cover close to Britain. The targets on this raid were the flak positions that can be seen burning beside the airfield runway in the lower part of the photo.
(David W. Fell and RAF Elsham Wolds Association)

A twin-engined night-fighter came diving down from above with its cannon firing. The German's shots went wide, but upper gunner Sergeant G. Relf was more accurate in his return fire. One of the engines on the enemy aircraft burst into flames as it shot past the bomber. The fire took hold and the aircraft continued its dive into a plummet towards the distant ground far below. Seconds later another night-fighter flashed past, without apparently attacking, but then a third fighter approached from the rear, all guns blazing. Rear gunner Sergeant T. Quinlan returned fire, pouring a long burst into the Focke Wulf 190 at almost point blank range. A wing on the German aircraft shattered at its root, making it two fighters to be marked up to the Lancaster. As the bomber powered through the skies towards home yet another fighter came in to attack. Again the gunners responded, but no hits were seen to either aircraft and the fighter vanished into the dark. Few crews can have had such a dramatic opening night.

Vernieuwe and his crew had an eventful tour of duty, adding a unique symbol to their Lancaster. All crews painted a bomb on the fuselage beside the cockpit to indicate missions completed, but Vernieuwe cheekily added a dinghy to M Mother. Returning from a raid on Kiel, he noticed a dinghy in the North Sea and went down to investigate. In the flimsy craft were seven men, clearly the crew of a downed Lancaster. Vernieuwe got his navigator to pinpoint the position, the radioed the location to Air Sea Rescue. When the drifting crew were rescued it turned out they had been adrift for almost a week on a fortuitously calm sea.

The entire crew led by Vernieuwe survived the war, with Tom Quinlan, the rear gunner, marrying a local girl and settling down near Elsham Wolds.

In September tragedy struck 625 Squadron at Kelstern. The Lancaster Q Queenie had just taken off loaded with bombs when an engine burst into flames. The pilot, Flying Officer Hannah, ordered his crew to bale out while he wrestled with the aircraft's controls. He narrowly managed to keep the doomed bomber clear of the village school, packed with local children, but could save neither the aircraft nor his own life. The bomber crashed into a field and blew up with a terrible blast.

One major effort in the autumn diverted Bomber Command from Germany. The mighty battleship *Tirpitz* was lurking in Tromsø Fjord in Norway. With her eight 15 inch guns and twelve 6 inch guns she was one of the most powerful battleships in the world. The Royal Navy was forced to keep three battleships on standby at all times ready to tackle her if she put to sea to attack the vital convoys crossing the Atlantic or travelling to Russia. Time and again convoys had been cancelled or turned back when the *Tirpitz* put to sea, or even fired up her engines. Without firing a shot the mighty battleship was disrupting the Allied war effort.

The Royal Navy wanted her sunk. The Fleet Air Arm made no fewer than nine attacks in the spring of 1944, but each time failed to sink the enemy ship. The Navy needed its battleships in the Pacific to wage the increasingly frenzied naval war against Japan, but could not move them

The memorial to 625 Squadron at Kelstern. This formation was formed in October 1943 and served in Lincolnshire to the end of hostilities. (http://www.oldairfields.fotopic.net/)

while the *Tirpitz* remained afloat. They asked the government for help.

In September 1944 Harris was summoned to the office of Prime Minister Churchill.

'Harris,' said Churchill, 'I want you to sink the *Tirpitz*.'

'But why bother?' replied Harris. 'She is not doing any harm sitting in that fjord.'

Churchill glared. 'Harris, I want you to sink the *Tirpitz*.'

Harris shrugged and set off back to his office. As ever when called upon to undertake a difficult task, he turned to his old command: 5 Group in Lincolnshire. The Group was still headed by Cochrane, so Harris put a call through. 'A job for 617, I suppose?' said Cochrane. Harris agreed. The Dambusters had a new task to perform.

The squadron was by this date commanded by Wing Commander James Tait, one of Harris's 'old lags'. Tait studied the maps and reports made by the crews of Fleet Air Arm who had already failed to hit the *Tirpitz*. Flak was heavy and accurate, while the ship was nestled in a deep, narrow section of the fjord. But the most effective defence was a metal pipe that ran around the fjord. At the flick of a switch, vast clouds of smoke billowed out of holes in the pipe. Within eight minutes the fjord was full of smoke and the battleship impossible to see.

Tait thought that the best attack method would be to roar in at 11,000 feet on full throttle, giving the bomb-aimers a chance to see the battleship as they approached so that they could get a fix. Even if the smoke came, Tait reasoned, bombs would be dropped on or near the ship. The attack took place on 15 September. As Tait hoped, his bomb-aimers sighted the ship clearly on the approach, but the smoke filled the valley more quickly than expected. The bombers dropped their bombs, but had no idea of how successful they had been. One bomber, with an all-Jewish crew, was lost on the return journey.

On the raid the squadron used a revolutionary new bomb, again designed by Barnes Wallis. This was the 'tallboy', a 12,000 lb monster that was superbly streamlined and encased in strengthened, highly polished steel. Dropped from 20,000 feet the bomb would have so much momentum by the time it reached the ground that it would slide into the earth and bury itself completely before exploding. The resulting blast would set up an earthquake effect that would literally shake any buildings to pieces, collapse underground structures and inflict massive damage on anything in the area. These 'tallboys' had been first used to collapse a crucial rail tunnel and block German reinforcements heading for Normandy in July 1944.

Now one of these giant bombs had plunged into the fjord only yards from the *Tirpitz*. When it exploded the 'tallboy' had lifted the ship up, then dropped it back down. The damage inflicted to the bottom of the ship was immense and would take months to repair. But the damage was invisible from the air, so it was missed by reconnaissance aircraft flown over to inspect the results of the raid. Cochrane told Tait that 617 Squadron would have to go back and complete the job.

At 1 am on 28 October 617 took off again, this time accompanied by 9 Squadron to make up a total of 36 Lancasters. Once again the smoke screen came up to meet the bombers as they thundered through the sky towards the *Tirpitz*. One 617 aircraft, piloted by Daniel Carey, went in lower than the rest. Carey was hoping to see something through the murk to enable an accurate bomb drop. Instead he was caught by a flak gun, which put a shell through his starboard wing and a second through his port wing. Two engines cut out instantly and fuel poured from the tanks.

He managed to pull the crippled Lancaster back into the air, clearing the mountains around the fjord by mere feet, then headed for Sweden. Carey crash-landed into a bog, but the crew got out alive.

Bad weather closed in and it was not until 12 November that 617 and 9 could have another attempt on the *Tirpitz*. Meanwhile, the Norwegian Resistance had sent an urgent message to London warning that 30 German fighter aircraft had arrived at Tromsø. The next attempt would be far more hazardous than before. Tait decided to attack in daylight nonetheless, to ensure accuracy.

The morning of the day the squadron was due to take off, Cochrane received an order from Bomber Command headquarters. A weapons expert was instructing the bombers to carry six smaller 2,000 lb bombs instead of a single 'tallboy', to improve the chances of a hit. Cochrane summoned his own bomb expert and asked his opinion. 'They'll never even dent her armour,' came the reply. 'But what can we do. It's an order.'

Cochrane flipped the order back on to his desk. 'We'll pop out for lunch,' he replied. 'I do hope I get back in time to pass this order on to Tait.' He didn't.

The Lancasters crossed the North Sea at low level to evade German radar, then climbed to 14,000 feet to give the 'tallboys' enough momentum to pierce the battleship's armour. As they climbed, the German radar picked them up and the fighters scrambled into the air. The *Tirpitz* came into sight, and stayed there. The smoke screen had developed a fault and did not work. Tait led 617 in first, and in such clear conditions they could scarcely miss. Ignoring the hail of flak that came up at them, the bomber pilots flew one after another over the ship. They scored four direct hits and twelve near misses. The battleship began to burn and, as the squadron wheeled away, her magazine blew up. The aircraft of 9 Squadron bombed into the smoke, but by then the *Tirpitz* was already finished. She turned over and capsized.

Minutes later dense banks of cloud rolled over the scene. The German fighters failed to find the Lancasters, all of which got back safely.

On 25 September, while 617 was concentrating on the *Tirpitz*, the rest of Bomber Command was given a new directive from the supreme command. This marked a major change in priorities. Instead of seeking to degrade the general industrial capacity of Germany, Bomber Command was now asked to concentrate on specific economic sectors. Prime among these was oil. On 20 August King Michael of Romania had taken his country out of the

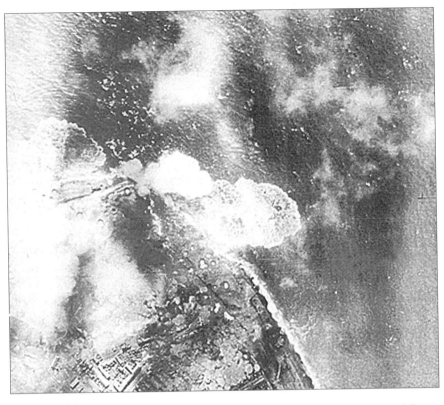

*A shot of Westkapelle taken during a raid on 3 October 1944 shows bombs falling
into the water and smoke obscuring much of the target.
(David W. Fell and RAF Elsham Wolds Association)*

war. The supplies of Romanian oil on which Germany had relied up until
then were suddenly cut off. To continue the war Germany now had only the
oil already stockpiled or the synthetic oil that could be produced from coal.
If these fuel sources could be knocked out, the panzers could not move, nor
could supplies be brought up to the front line. Secondary targets included
weapons factories, airbases, rail junctions and road bridges.

The directive recognised that such specific targets could be hit only
on clear nights by specially trained squadrons. The majority of Bomber
Command's efforts continued to be directed against general industrial
towns. For the men flying the missions there was little change at all.
Whatever their targets might be, reaching them still involved long flights
through the heavily-defended night skies over the Reich.

The men of Bomber Command did, however, have some improvements on their side. The first was the new 'GH' system. This was a better version of 'Gee' that enabled a navigator to determine his position with much greater accuracy almost anywhere over Germany. The second advantage that came increasingly to the fore was the fact that Allied armies were advancing through France. Instead of being faced by the dread decision of whether to bale out or risk setting off across the North Sea, the crews of damaged bombers could now head for friendly airbases in France. Losses fell as stricken bombers were able to struggle to safety.

By October the bombing campaign on Germany was reaching its height. Forces of 500 to 700 heavy bombers were becoming usual in heavy raids and the damage they inflicted on target cities was frightful. Entire areas were laid waste as thousands of buildings were reduced to rubble by the concentrated assault with high explosives and incendiaries.

As before, it was the industrial cities producing war supplies that took the brunt of the offensive. Stuttgart was targeted on the night of 21 October 1944, with 153 Squadron from Scampton putting up their full strength. One aircraft was piloted by Flying Officer Don Freeborn. As he began his bombing run the sudden blast of a flak shell bursting slightly to port temporarily blinded him. At first he thought he had been deafened too, then realised he had merely jerked the intercom lead from its socket. He did realise that he had been badly wounded in the left thigh. Plugging his intercom back in, Freeborn was about to announce his injury when he heard the steady voice of the bomb-aimer giving him instructions. Reasoning that if the rest of the crew could ignore such a near miss, he should as well, Freeborn flew on to complete the bomb drop.

Only as they cleared Stuttgart did Freeborn inform his crew about his wound, at which point he realised that none of them had even noticed the flak burst. The bomb-aimer tried to give first aid, but Freeborn's leg was so tightly pushed against the fuselage side that he could not reach it, and Freeborn could not move out of the seat as it had been damaged in the blast and his harness would not unclip. Freeborn himself had roughly to attach a dressing while his comrade held the control column.

Despite his wounds, and the increasingly severe pain, Freeborn flew the Lancaster back to an emergency landing strip at Manston, in Kent. The stress Freeborn was under can be judged by the fact that as the Lancaster rolled to a gentle halt on landing, he passed out completely and did not recover his senses until two days later in hospital. He was given an immediate DFC.

Messerschmitt Bf110G

Type:	Night-fighter
Engines:	2 x 1,475 hp Daimler-Benz DB605B-1
Wingspan:	53 ft 3 in
Length:	39 ft 7 in
Height:	13 ft 8 in
Weight:	Empty 11,220 lb
	Loaded 21,799 lb
Armament:	2 x 20 mm cannon and 4 x 7.9 mm machine guns in fixed forward firing position, plus 2 x 7.9 mm machine guns in rear cockpit
Max speed:	342 mph
Ceiling:	26,000 ft
Range:	560 miles
Production:	3,650

The Messerschmitt Bf110 had proved disappointing in its designated role as a long-range fighter during the Battle of Britain in 1940 and production was being wound down when the worth of the new night-fighter model G became clear with the increasing numbers of night raids by the RAF. Production was increased to meet demand, and the aircraft was produced in a number of variants as radar and weaponry were constantly updated and improved. By the time production was halted in February 1945 about 15 versions of the Bf110G had entered combat.

Chapter 9

The Final
Battles

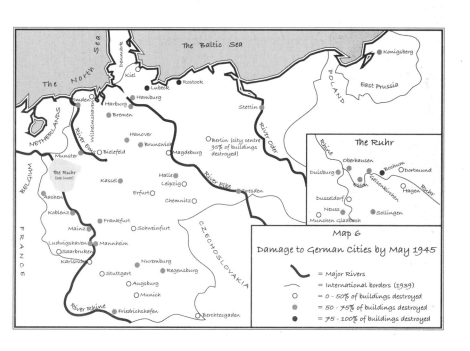

Map 6
Damage to German Cities by May 1945

= Major Rivers
= International borders (1939)
○ = 0 - 50% of buildings destroyed
◉ = 50 - 75% of buildings destroyed
● = 75 - 100% of buildings destroyed

A raid on Cologne on 31 October showed up two of the routine hazards encountered by the crews of Bomber Command, and both happened to aircraft of 153 Squadron.

Just after take off, Squadron Leader Gee found that his airspeed indicator was not working. The navigator was able to guide the aircraft to Cologne and back more or less on schedule, but the real danger came on landing. Gee tried to gauge his speed, but darkness covered the landscape and it was not until he touched down that he realised he was going far too quickly. The brakes were jammed on full, but even so the heavy bomber missed a building only narrowly and shuddered to a halt just feet from the perimeter fence.

Meanwhile, over Cologne, the Lancaster A Apple piloted by Flying Officer Wheeler suddenly veered savagely to starboard. Thinking a flak shell might have burst under the port wing, Wheeler peered out, but could see no obvious damage. He continued to bomb on target, then turned for home. At this point an ashen-faced wireless operator came into the cockpit in a clear state of distress. 'Skipper,' he said, 'the starboard wing's damaged.'

Wheeler now looked out the other side of the cockpit to see a gaping hole over a yard across in the centre of the starboard wing. The wireless operator then reported that he had taken up his usual position in the small perspex dome in the top of the fuselage, the astrodome, to keep an eye out for the risk of collision with other bombers in the closely packed stream. He had glanced up to see an entire stick of 1,000 lb bombs hurtling down seemingly straight at him. 'I was too paralysed to speak,' he confessed. Most of the bombs missed A Apple, but one had hit the wing. Wheeler got his aircraft back safely.

The Lancaster Q Queenie piloted by Flying Officer Williams completed the Cologne mission without incident, but on coming in to land before dawn the aircraft suddenly lurched upward and sideways. Only with great skill did Williams regain control of the bomber in time to put it down on the runway. Having parked the bomber, the crew climbed out to find leaves and twigs jammed in the undercarriage. Clearly Williams had clipped the top of a tree, unseen in the darkness.

Such were the dangers faced by the crews of Bomber Command, even when the Germans were not trying to kill them.

In December weeks of dreadful weather closed in over Europe. Major raids were few and far between. The Germans took advantage of the bad weather to launch their offensive through the Ardennes that came to be known as the

Battle of the Bulge. Although the initial breakthrough was impressive, the attack foundered due to a combination of determined American resistance at key points, and a lack of fuel for German motorised columns. It was a quiet end to the year for the men flying from Lincolnshire.

In January 1945 the skies over Europe cleared for the first time in weeks. Bomber Command was ready to return to the offensive. The Luftwaffe was also ready for the renewed struggle. As well as the uprated Messerschmitt 110 models, they could also deploy the jet-fighter Messerschmitt Me262, codenamed 'Schwalbe' or 'Swallow'. The new fighter was horribly effective in shooting down bombers and became a dreaded nightmare for the crews of Bomber Command. Fortunately few of these magnificent aircraft were completed before the war ended.

The cause of another worrying feature of night flying over the Reich at this time has remained a mystery. Bomber crews were reporting that their larger formations were being accompanied by small glowing balls of light. These seemed to be circular aircraft that kept pace with the bombers, occasionally diving, climbing or changing direction. At first they were thought to be German weapons or remotely controlled monitoring equipment of some kind. The crews dubbed them 'foo-fighters' and tried to shoot them down. None seem to have been damaged by gunfire and soon the crews gave up trying to damage this strange craft. After the war, studies of the German files showed that they were just as mystified by the 'foo-fighters' as were the British and thought they must be some kind of navigational aid flown by the British. What they really were has never been discovered.

The first raid of the new year began when U Uncle, a Lancaster of 9 Squadron, took off from Bardney before dawn on 1 January 1945 to join an attack on the Dortmund-Ems Canal. Seconds after the bombs were let go, two flak shells exploded very close to the bomber. The first tore a massive hole in the floor of the aircraft, just in front of the upper turret, and started a fire. The second tore off the nose of the aircraft, shattered the cockpit canopy and set the port inner engine on fire. The pilot, Harry Denton, set off the engine extinguisher and struggled to get the aircraft under control.

Meanwhile the wireless operator, George Thompson, had noticed that the upper gunner was making no attempt to escape from his turret despite the flames below him. Thompson began moving down the fuselage only to encounter the gaping hole in the floor. Nothing daunted, Thompson climbed along the wall of the fuselage, hanging on to its ribs and fastenings. Reaching the turret, he found that the gunner, Ernie Potts, was alive but

Flying Officer Edward Saslove lost his life during a raid on Munich when he tried to save the lives of most of his crew. (David W. Fell and RAF Elsham Wolds Association)

unconscious. Thompson unbuckled the gunner's harness and pulled him from the turret. Slinging the senseless man on his shoulder, he then climbed back over the hole to safety in the front of the fuselage.

Meanwhile the rear gunner, Haydn Price, had tried to bale out, but found that a sheet of flame was rushing out of the bomber directly beneath his turret. He opened the door, but got badly burned, so closed it again. He was wondering what to do next when the door to his turret opened to reveal a badly burned Thompson who had fought his way past the broken fuselage a second time and rushed through the flames to reach Price. He led Price back through the fire and past the broken hole to join Potts. All three men had lost their parachutes to the fire.

With three men unable to bale out, Denton decided to try to reach Allied lines, now in Belgium. As the crippled bomber flew west he was appalled to see a formation of Messerschmitts heading straight at him. Fortunately a squadron of Spitfires then appeared and drove the Germans away. Two of the Spitfires peeled off from their own mission to escort the bomber back to an emergency landing strip at Eindhoven.

The bomber was too damaged to make it. Realising this, Denton chose a large field and put the Lancaster down in a belly landing. The shock of impact broke off the tail of the aircraft and the wreckage skidded to halt beside an earthen bank. The crew dragged themselves and each other out of the tangled wreck to await assistance. The Spitfire pilots had radioed their position and soon two ambulances arrived.

Sadly Potts died next day, but the others recovered. Thompson himself had been badly weakened by his injuries, so when he caught pneumonia it proved to be fatal. He died just days before it was announced that he had been awarded a Victoria Cross for his actions.

Equally selfless was the courage of Canadian volunteer Edward Saslove. On the night of the 7/8 January the largely Canadian crew of Flying Officer Edward Saslove took off from Fiskerton with the rest of 576 Squadron to bomb Munich. The crew had been together for 12 missions and was recognised as one of the most tightly knit in the squadron. Unfortunately as the aircraft was turning away from the target it was attacked by a night-fighter. The damage to the Lancaster was such that it would clearly not get back to England. Two engines had been knocked out and a small fire was burning in the fuselage. Both the rear and upper gunners were wounded and unable to bale out.

Saslove ordered his four uninjured crew to bale out. As the last of them prepared to jump through the escape hatch he turned to look at Saslove. The pilot waved cheerfully, then faced back to the controls. The four men parachuted to safety, but sadly Saslove and his gunners did not escape. The aircraft went out of control and crashed into a field near Munich. Saslove could easily have engaged the automatic pilot and baled out, but he chose to try to save the lives of his comrades rather than save his own.

In the autumn of 1944 something that is probably unique was achieved by 103 Squadron. Two brothers, John Henry and David Henry, were both pilots with the squadron when their younger brother, Gavin Henry, gained his wings and was posted to the same squadron. The three had grown up in the remote outback township of Armidale, New South Wales, and had volunteered for pilot training. During their time at the squadron, John was referred to as Henry Mk1, being the eldest, while David was Henry Mk2 and Gavin was Henry Mk3.

In February 1945 the two elder brothers had completed 29 missions and were preparing to undertake their final flights of their first tour while young Gavin had flown only 10 missions. Together they asked the squadron commander if they could all fly on the next raid so that they would have flown one mission together. The request was turned down flat as the RAF had a firm policy of never allowing brothers to take part in the

The crew for which Saslove gave his life.
(David W. Fell and RAF Elsham Wolds Association)

The famous Henry Brothers, who hit the national newspaper headlines in the spring of 1945 when they all piloted Lancasters on the same raid against Cologne. (David W. Fell and RAF Elsham Wolds Association)

same mission. The Henry boys were, however, insistent and demanded that the request should be passed up to Group Headquarters.

The commanding officer of 5 Group was by this time the same Hugh Constantine who had enthusiastically left his desk to pilot a bomber on the first of the Thousand Bomber Raids. He was sympathetic to the request, but felt unable to agree, whereupon the brothers promptly wrote to King George VI himself. The king sent an officer of the royal household to Elsham Wolds to interview the young brothers and make sure that they were really keen to go and were not being pressured into the mission. Satisfied, the king agreed.

And so it was that all three brothers piloted a Lancaster each on a raid to Cologne. They all came home safely and, indeed, survived the war.

The Amos brothers were not so fortunate. They hailed from Ashford,

Sergeant Albert Amos who, with his brothers, served in Bomber Command.
(David W. Fell and RAF Elsham Wolds Association)

Kent, and all joined the RAF early in the war. In July 1943 Elmer, who was a flight engineer with 103 Squadron, was killed in action. Albert, then undertaking ground crew duties in the Middle East, at once volunteered to take his place. At this time the RAF had a shortage of flight engineers and when Albert volunteered for this duty he was

Albert Amos and the crew with which he volunteered to fly extra missions in 1945. (David W. Fell and RAF Elsham Wolds Association)

accepted and returned to the UK on 15 October 1943.

On completion of his flight engineer's training Albert joined the crew of Flying Officer A. McNeill with 166 Squadron at Kirmington on 10 August 1944. The crew's 15th mission was to Duisberg, but Albert was ill and his place was taken by Sergeant W.G. Angles. Sadly the bomber was shot down

183

and all killed. Albert was transferred to 576 Squadron to join the crew of Flight Lieutenant G.A. Campbell. As a 'spare', Albert also flew with other crews and in April 1945 he completed his tour of 30 operations. Campbell and his crew had not, so Albert volunteered to continue flying with them until they had reached their 30th mission. Their final mission came on 22 April 1945 with a daylight raid on Bremen in preparation for the assault on the city by the British XXX Corps.

Amos remained in the RAF after the war, pausing only to return to Ashford to marry his sweetheart Sylvia Farmer in 1946. He later served with 617 Squadron and left the RAF in 1950, though he remained in the reserves until 1959.

The bombing campaign of early 1945 was proceeding to complete the objectives set in the autumn of 1944. Oil installations were the priority target, followed by transportation and armaments factories. But in February

In the dying months of the conflict, a Lancaster bomber drops a tallboy bomb during the raid on the Bielfeld viaduct, a vital link in Germany's transport network. Only these enormously powerful 'earthquake' bombs were able to destroy such targets.

1945 a new directive was issued. The Soviet Red Army was now marching into Germany, but was suffering heavy losses inflicted by determined German resistance. The Soviets had long concentrated on ground support bombers that were light or medium, and had no heavy bomber force to speak of. Stalin personally asked Churchill if the RAF could bomb strategic targets in eastern Germany that lay in the path of the Red Army.

The targets highlighted were primarily rail junctions, road bridges and administrative centres in cities such as Stettin, Chemnitz and Dresden. These cities had not been heavily bombed before. This was partly because to attack them involved long flights through heavily defended skies and partly because they did not contain a concentration of targets that would make area bombing effective. Now they were to be hit, and hit hard, though Bomber Command never let up on the targets closer to home.

It was on a raid against Hanover on 15 March that one of the most bizarre incidents of the entire war fought by Bomber Command from Lincolnshire took place. Flying Officer Ted Parker was piloting Lancaster A Apple of 153 Squadron. The flight out was without incident and Hanover came into sight with the target markers falling from the Pathfinders far ahead. Correcting his course slightly to aim his aircraft directly at the target, Parker was about to call up his bomb-aimer on the intercom when it happened.

He was suddenly all alone and falling through the night sky. The Lancaster had gone. Parker was on his own in the darkness, with the deep silence of the night broken only by the sound of the air rushing past his ears. Parker pulled his ripcord and the parachute opened. He then found time to look around. He could see no flak, no night-fighter and, strangest of all, no sign of his own aircraft. Neither Parker nor anyone else was ever able to explain what had happened.

Two nights later 153 Squadron was back over Germany and this time it was the aircraft flown by Flying Officer Joe Sharp that encountered a mystery, though this was solved. Over the target the starboard outer engine suddenly burst into flames. Flight engineer David Broughton hurriedly checked the instruments, but they showed that nothing was wrong and that the engine was working normally. Nevertheless, flames streamed out yards behind the aircraft so the engine was switched off. The fire gradually died down and went out, allowing the bomber to fly home on three engines. After landing back at Scampton, the crew inspected the blackened engine. As the instruments had shown, there was nothing wrong with it.

It was only later as the ground crew stripped the engine down that the

The damage wrought on German industrial cities by Bomber Command was frightful. The city centre of Cologne, shown here in June 1945, had 95% of its buildings destroyed.

mystery was solved. A few fragments of an incendiary bomb were found. Clearly the bomb had fallen from a Lancaster higher up and been sucked into the cowling. It was the bomb, not the engine that had been on fire. Sharp could have restarted the engine at any time he chose.

In early April 1945 reconnaissance aircraft were taking photographs that showed quite clearly that Bomber Command was close to having achieved its prime purpose. The industrial capacity of Germany to wage war was almost destroyed. Factories were no longer producing weapons, oil installations were no longer producing oil and what could be produced was unable to reach the front line due to destroyed communication links. The vast fleet of heavy bombers had little left to do other than pound the remaining German battlefield defences.

One mission that Harris did devise was among the most spectacular of the war. At the time nobody was certain from which lair Hitler was directing the final stages of the conflict. It was known, however, that the SS was preparing to conduct a guerrilla war and that the base for this operation was in southern Germany. This led Harris to conclude that Hitler himself was in southern Germany. The only known command headquarters was at Berchtesgaden, Hitler's mountain lodge, where there was also a major SS camp.

On 25 April 375 bombers set off in daylight to bomb Berchtesgaden. No fighters came up to challenge the formation as it pushed over the once-mighty Reich. The target was obliterated, but Hitler was not there. He was in Berlin where he would soon commit suicide.

Even when the war ended on 3 May, Bomber Command's work was not over. The mighty bombers were hurriedly converted to transports and used to fly home liberated prisoners of war. Among the squadrons taking part in this 'Operation Exodus' was 153. Pilot Bill Langford landed at Brussels to pick up a load of returning prisoners. Langford was a popular character who had painted small tankards of

The imposing statue of 'Bomber' Harris that stands outside St Clement Danes church in London. The statue is dedicated to all the men of Bomber Command as well as to Harris.

In 1986 the Post Office issued a commemorative series of stamps celebrating the 50th anniversary of the reorganisation the RAF. This First Day Cover pays particular attention to Arthur Harris, and was the first post-war celebration of his role in achieving final victory.

foaming beer on his aircraft in place of the more usual bombs.

While Langford was in the airport office completing his paperwork, a group of prisoners wandered around looking at the bombers. One group was the crew of a Hampden shot down in 1941. They gazed in awe at the huge aircraft, so much larger than those they had flown. They chuckled at the painted beer mugs and one remarked: 'That's just the sort of thing my kid brother would do. He always liked his beer.' Astonishingly the man was Richard Langford, Bill's elder brother. Although they were only yards apart, the two men did not meet at Brussels but were reunited some weeks later in England.

Other bombers flew badly needed supplies of food to Holland and areas that were suffering shortages. After the work of destruction, the work of peace came as a welcome change.

Barnes Wallis – who had invented the Wellington, the bouncing bomb and the 'tallboy' among many other developments – was awarded a cash bonus of £10,000 for his wartime work. In the 1940s that was a colossal sum of money, and most agreed that it was richly deserved. He accepted the money gratefully, then at once donated the entire amount to a fund set up to help the children of RAF men killed during the war. There were many of them.

Throughout the war the men of Bomber Command in Lincolnshire faced daunting odds. Their chances of surviving a tour of 30 operations was about 50%, that of completing the officially required two tours was barely one in three. And the disproportionate risk to inexperienced crews meant that most deaths came to crew members on their first five missions. It was a horrible casualty rate that led to the deaths of some 55,500 aircrew from Bomber Command during the war. Another 9,000 were wounded badly enough to need hospital treatment and almost 10,000 were shot down and captured by the Germans.

And yet morale never faltered. These men were heroes indeed.

Even today the remains of Bomber Command crews are being found as the wreckage of their aircraft is recovered across Germany and Europe. This funeral for five aircrew, was attended by an RAF bugler and colour party. It was held at Oueilly in 1999.

Index

*The magnificent gilded
eagle that tops the
RAF Monument on the
Embankment in central
London.*